Reading Activities

CONTRIBUTING WRITERS:
Marilee Robin Burton
Beth Alley Wise
Suzanne I. Barchers, Ed.D.

CONTRIBUTING CONSULTANTS:
Leslie Anne Perry, Ph.D.
Susan Miller, Ph.D.
Elizabeth Crosby Stull, Ph.D.

Publications International, Ltd.

Contributing Writers:

Marilee Robin Burton is an educational writer, consultant, and language-arts specialist. She has more than ten years experience as a teacher and has contributed to *365 Reading Activities, Parenting Magazine, Early Childhood Today, Creative Classroom,* and other publications. She holds a master's degree in early childhood education and human development.

Beth Alley Wise is an early-childhood-education specialist and the author of over 50 children's books, including *Beginning to Read, Key Words to Reading,* and *My Reading Kit.* She has written and edited textbooks and software for numerous publishers and serves as a developmental specialist on reading reforms.

Suzanne I. Barchers, Ed.D., has written numerous books and articles on reading, language arts, and literacy for children. She serves as an affiliate faculty member at the University of Colorado, Denver, and has been an educator, reading specialist, and administrator at public and private schools in Denver.

Contributing Consultants:

Leslie Anne Perry, Ph.D., has been Assistant Professor for the Department of Curriculum and Instruction at East Tennessee State University. She has a Ph.D. in elementary education with a specialization in reading and a masters degree in early childhood education. She has contributed to several books on reading for educators, and her articles have appeared in various educational publications.

Susan Miller, Ph.D., has been a professor of early childhood education at the university level. She has written more than 150 books and journal and magazine articles, including Scholastic's *Early Childhood Today, Childhood Education,* and *Early Childhood News.* Miller is a frequent presenter at conferences sponsored by the National Association for the Education of Young Children and the Association of Childhood Education International Study.

Elizabeth Crosby Stull, Ph.D., has been Assistant Professor of Language and Literacy, Children's Literature, at Ohio State University. She has written several books, including curriculum activity guides for The Center for Applied Research in Education, and is a member of the International Reading Association and the National Association for Education of Young Children.

Contributing Illustrators:
Terri and Joe Chicko, Kate Flanagan, and Lynn Sweat

Louis Weber, CEO
Publications International, Ltd.
7373 North Cicero Avenue
Lincolnwood, Illinois 60712

Permission is never granted for commercial purposes.

Manufactured in China.

8 7 6 5 4 3 2 1

ISBN: 0-7853-4472-1

Contents

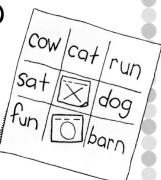

The Joy of Reading

The title *Reading Activities* suggests this book is limited only to the activity of reading. As anyone who's ever taught a child to read understands, reading is not that simple. It incorporates a variety of language-arts skills. This book is full of appealing activities that explore an array of skills in exciting, motivating, and educational ways. All of these projects and activities will contribute to your child's reading development.

Reading, writing, listening, and speaking are the four major areas of language arts—each reinforces the others. Activities that focus on writing, listening, and speaking, therefore, develop and reinforce skills that are necessary for reading success. From word webs and pic-ture dictionaries to storytelling and creative writing, the activities in this book will help your child become a more confident reader.

To obtain a full learning experience, your child will require your help with these activities. Take the time to go over the instructions for each activity carefully with your child, have patience, and be free in your use of encouragement and praise.

Book symbols near the title of each activity identify the level of difficulty: Three books identify challenging activities; two books indicate intermediate activities; and one book marks relatively easy activities. Keep in mind when choosing activities that children learn at different rates. An activity that one child finds easy may be more challenging for another child of the same age. Regardless of the age of your child, you may want to start with a few of the easier activities and work up in difficulty. Some activities, such as those using scissors or other implements, require close adult supervision for safety reasons. Be sure to read all the instructions carefully and adhere to any words of caution.

Each of this book's six chapters focuses on a different element of reading and language arts and contains a wide variety of activities designed to enhance a particular skill. Chapter 1, "Comprehension Capers," helps the child make sense of what he or she is reading. This chapter offers activities intended to generate the child's enthusiasm for reading while building skills necessary for comprehension and understanding.

Although the title of Chapter 2 is "Alphabet Adventures," it provides more than just your ABC's. Reading requires children to recognize letters and the sounds they make, so this chapter includes activities about spelling and phonics, as well.

Chapter 3, "Celebrating Stories," shifts the focus to combining words and ideas in the act of storytelling. Some activities will help your child understand how stories are put together, while others will encourage the child to create stories on his or her own.

"Vocabulary Views," Chapter 4, focuses on expanding vocabulary. Further, the child will explore different aspects of vocabulary words, such as their division into syllables or their rhyming relationship to other words.

Words, of course, are the building blocks of language and reading. Chapter 5, "Words and More Words," offers even more word identification games. These activities will engage your child in lively word play while improving basic vocabulary skills.

The final chapter, "Ready for Writing," presents activities to strengthen and

reinforce reading skills through poems, letters, and other writing exercises. Reading and writing are simply two heads of the same coin, of course. The competent writer usually excels at reading and vice versa.

The activities presented here are not in any particular order, so feel free to skip around in the book. If your child responds to one type of activity, such as looking at pictures in magazines, then you may want to suggest more such activities. The index makes finding similar activities simple.

You play a critical role in your child's reading development. In effect, you are your child's first teacher. With your guidance, and with the activities contained in this book, your child will grow in competence and confidence as he or she embarks on one of life's most wondrous and rewarding adventures—reading!

Chapter 1
Comprehension Capers

Hoop It Up

Hoop it up with this sockball-tossing game of skill, poetry, and real or make-believe story events.

What You'll Need:

masking tape

2 small waste-baskets

paper

markers

storybooks

balled-up socks

Before beginning, mark a line on the floor with masking tape. Place two small waste-baskets about 12 feet from the line. Tape labels marked "REAL" and "MAKE-BELIEVE" on the sides of the wastebaskets. Set out a pile of balled-up socks by the masking-tape line.

To play, invite the child to read favorite passages from books or poems he or she recently read or enjoyed. Ask the child to decide whether the events and characters are real or make-believe. Allow time for the child to answer. Once an answer is given, have the child stand behind the line and toss a balled-up sock into the appropriate basket. When all the socks have been tossed, count them to see how many characters or events the child thought were real and how many were make-believe.

Blast Off!

10–9–8–7–6–5–4–3–2–1 BLAST OFF into reading comprehension with this rocket-construction project.

What You'll Need:

blue construction paper

scissors

tape

cardboard toilet paper roll

pencil

white paper cut into long strips

Cut a 6-inch circle out of blue construction paper, and cut a pie-shaped wedge from it. Then wrap and tape the paper circle to make a cone. Tape the cone to the top of the cardboard tube.

Next invite the child to write the main idea of a favorite story on the body of the cardboard-tube rocket. If you prefer, the child can use a personal experience as a basis for the main idea. Help the child write supporting details on the strips of white paper. Then have the child tape the strips of paper to the bottom of the rocket.

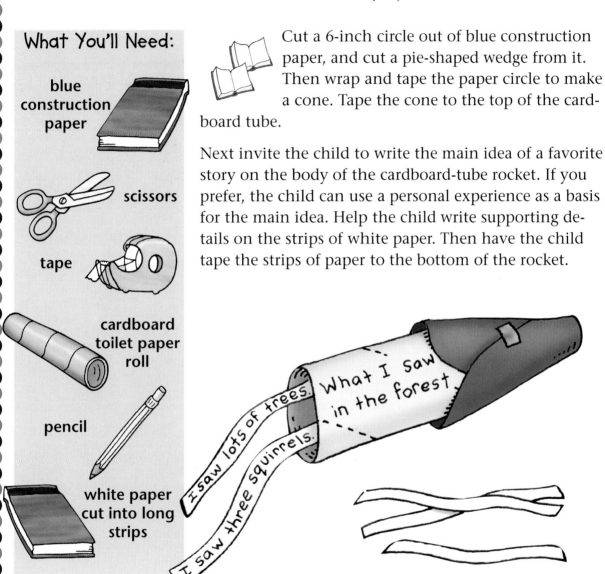

Lost and Found

Where, oh where, has my favorite storybook character gone?

What You'll Need:

storybooks

posterboard

crayons or markers

 Place a collection of favorite storybooks on a reading table or in another quiet reading area in the house, and provide ample time for the child to browse through the books before you begin this activity.

Tell the child that a character in one of the storybooks is lost, and invite the child to make a "lost and found" poster for that character. Let the child pick the character who is lost. Encourage the child to describe the lost character before beginning to draw. Explain that the reader will want to know who is lost, what the character looks like, and anything else about the character that would help identify that character. Invite the child to return to the

book area, if needed, to look for pictures of the selected character or to double-check information.

As the child works on the poster, make sure he or she includes information about what should be done if the lost character is found. Encourage creative thinking and spontaneity as the child creates the poster.

Envelope Puppets

An imaginative child will love creating these animated story puppets.

What You'll Need:

6½×9½-inch manila envelopes

scissors

markers

glue or clear tape

arts and crafts scraps

Set out all materials. Use as many envelopes as the number of puppets you and the child intend to make. To make a puppet, carefully cut off the top flap of a manila envelope. This open end will be the bottom of the puppet. Invite the child to draw a face on the envelope. Have the child glue or tape odds and ends of arts and crafts scraps on the envelope to create a puppet resembling a character from a favorite story or book. The child can make puppets for every character involved in the story he or she wants to tell. Have the child put his or her hands inside the envelope puppets. Encourage the child to use the finished puppets for retelling the story or for other dramatic play.

For an additional activity, help the child create a puppet stage. Paint a cardboard box with poster paints, and use it as the setting of the story.

Picture Reading

This activity is sure to help a beginning reader get excited about reading.

What You'll Need:

illustrated book

sticky notes

 Choose an illustrated book that has words the child uses when talking or playing. Each page of the book should have just one or two words. A book the child is already familiar with and enjoys, such as a book about toys or animals, would be particularly useful.

Cover one of the words on a page with a sticky note. Have the child describe the illustration. Then remove the sticky note, and compare the child's description of the illustration to the text. If the child used a word that is a good description but different than the word in the book, discuss how different words can sometimes be used to describe what is happening in an illustration.

What Will Happen?

As with all skills, making accurate predictions takes practice. Try it and see!

What You'll Need:

paper

pencil

 Before you and the child go shopping, run errands, or visit friends of family, discuss what you might see and hear and what might happen. Make a list of your predictions. After returning from your outing, check the list and see how many of the predictions were accurate.

Totem Poles

Learn about other cultures and traditions while building totem poles that reflect important images from a story.

What You'll Need:

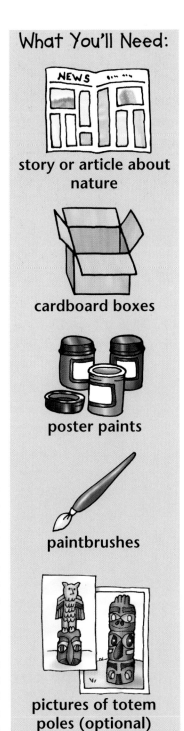

story or article about nature

cardboard boxes

poster paints

paintbrushes

pictures of totem poles (optional)

 Explain to the child that a totem pole is a tall pole on which animals and other images from nature are carved or painted. Explain that totem poles are symbolic and often tell a story. If possible, show the child examples of authentic Native American totem poles from picture books.

Invite the child to read a nonfiction story or article about animals or nature. Then help the child paint cardboard boxes depicting important images from the story. Allow plenty of time for the boxes to dry before moving them. Finally, have the child stack the boxes so that they resemble a totem pole.

Fingerpaint Follies

These tasty substitutes for fingerpaint provide an easy-to-clean-up and fun-to-use method to paint predictions.

What You'll Need:

ready-made pudding or whipped cream

smock

nursery rhyme

sponges

Invite the child to spread the whipped cream or ready-made pudding on the top of a clean kitchen table, preferably one with a surface that can be cleaned easily with sponges and water. Make sure the child is wearing a smock so he or she can be easily cleaned as well. Then read a nursery rhyme that is unfamiliar to the child. At some point in the rhyme, pause and ask the child to finger-paint a picture showing what he or she predicts will happen next.

Repeat this activity with other nursery rhymes. Have the child "erase" the previous drawing by rubbing over it with his or her hands. When finished, the child can sponge the excess whipped cream off the table.

Pop, Pop, Popcorn!

Put the child's senses through a vocabulary test with this popping good activity.

What You'll Need:

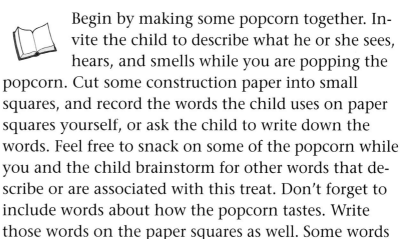

popcorn

popcorn popper

construction paper

scissors

pencil

threaded needle

Begin by making some popcorn together. Invite the child to describe what he or she sees, hears, and smells while you are popping the popcorn. Cut some construction paper into small squares, and record the words the child uses on paper squares yourself, or ask the child to write down the words. Feel free to snack on some of the popcorn while you and the child brainstorm for other words that describe or are associated with this treat. Don't forget to include words about how the popcorn tastes. Write those words on the paper squares as well. Some words you might want to include are *salty, crunchy, pop, hot, white, munch,* and *yummy.*

Next help the child use the needle to string some of the popcorn, together with the words on paper squares, along the thread to create a decorative word bank. Display the completed popcorn-and-word strand in the room for a day or so to review the words. Then remove the popcorn from the strand, and take it outside for birds to enjoy.

Riddle Dee Dee

The child strengthens comprehension skills while hopping through riddles.

What You'll Need:

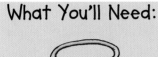

3–5 hula hoops

riddle book

Lay the hula hoops on the floor, one in front of the other, as shown in the illustration. Read a riddle, and invite the child to solve it. For a correct answer, the child can hop into the first hula hoop. If the child is unable to answer the riddle, however, he or she cannot advance and must wait for the next riddle. Keep asking riddles until the child has reached the last hula hoop. Once the child does reach the end, switch roles and allow the child to ask the riddles while you progress through the hoops.

Back-to-Back Pictures

This exercise helps the child learn to interpret verbal information through drawings.

What You'll Need:

paper

crayons

Set up a seating arrangement in which you and the child each have a piece of paper but cannot see the other person's paper. Choose a common object, and begin to draw a picture of it. As you are drawing, describe your picture, and have the child draw according to your description. Don't share the drawings until you are both finished. When the drawings are complete, compare them to see how well the child matched your description. Try another set of drawings, this time with the child describing his or her drawing to you.

Travel Poster

Visit faraway countries, interesting cities, or other travel destinations without leaving home. Here's how.

What You'll Need:

old magazines

scissors

scrap art materials

posterboard

clear tape or glue

markers

 Help the child think of words that can describe nouns. Explain that these descriptive words are called "adjectives." Next invite the child to make a travel poster that encourages his or her friends to visit a new place. The travel destination may be a place the child has actually visited or a place he or she would like to travel to one day. It may be a country, state, city, or specific tourist attraction.

To make the travel poster, look through old magazines, and help the child cut out pictures of sights a traveler would want to see while visiting a chosen destination. The child could also make

inviting pictures from scrap art materials. Tape or glue the pictures on the posterboard. Remember, the pictures should describe the location in a way that would motivate others to travel there. Once the pictures have been placed, have the child write phrases using colorful adjectives that describe the destination. Find a place where the poster can be easily seen, and put it on display.

Dramatic Diorama

Use this activity to bring a favorite story to life!

What You'll Need:

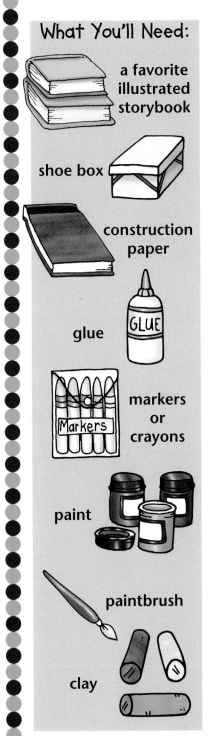

a favorite illustrated storybook

shoe box

construction paper

glue

markers or crayons

paint

paintbrush

clay

 Read a favorite story aloud and discuss the illustrations together. The more vivid and exotic the illustrations are, the better. Use the illustrations to inspire a diorama, which is a three-dimensional representation of a scene, and make the diorama together.

Begin by choosing one long side of the inside of the shoe box to be the bottom when the box is turned on its side. Decide what color the bottom  should be, and get construction paper to match that color. For instance, if the ground will be made up of grass, use green construction paper. If it will be water, use blue construction paper. You can also draw or color on the construction paper to add different elements, such as a sidewalk or path. Then cover the remaining sides with blue construction paper for the sky. If appropriate, the child can draw clouds or birds in the sky.

To construct the inside, turn the shoe box on its side, with the side you chose for the bottom down. Talk with the child about what should be included in the diorama: trees, grass, buildings, cars, boats, and anything else you think of. Invite the child to use construction paper, markers or crayons, and paint to create these objects. Use clay to fashion any people or animals you want to include. Display the diorama next to the book it illustrates. Then use the diorama when retelling or rereading the story.

Opening a Can of Worms

The child will wiggle and giggle while learning about main ideas and supporting details.

What You'll Need:

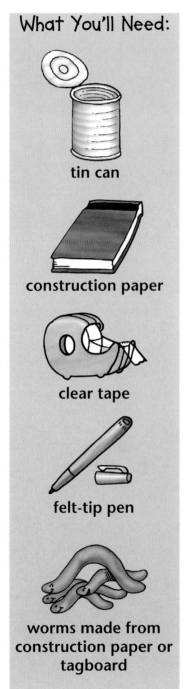

tin can

construction paper

clear tape

felt-tip pen

worms made from
construction paper or
tagboard

Begin by wrapping a tin can (with a smooth edge) with construction paper and securing it with tape. Write the main idea of a familiar story on the outside of the tin can, turning the can around so the child will not see it. On each paper worm, write a supporting detail of the story, then place all the worms in the can. Explain that supporting details are pieces of information that work together to help tell the main idea. You may also want to discuss how each story has a beginning, a middle, and an end. Invite the child to pick worms from the can, read the sentences on them, and identify the main idea of the story.

The Bear Saw Lots of Animals

Radio Advertising

Learn how to advertise a favorite book on the radio!

What You'll Need:

favorite book

paper

pencil

tape recorder

Invite the child to reread a favorite book. Discuss what the child likes about the book and what makes it outstanding. Then help the child create an ad appropriate for reading on the radio. It should truly "sell" the book to listeners. Write down the ad. Then have the child practice reading it into a tape recorder until it is ready to be shared.

Cliff-Hangers

The child will enjoy reading a good cliff-hanger while practicing reading and comprehension skills.

What You'll Need:

book with multiple chapters

tape recorder

Read a "cliff-hanger" story into a tape recorder. Then have the child listen to the tape and read in the book along with it. This will help the child follow and understand the text. After each chapter, stop the tape recorder, and invite the child to predict what will happen next. Discuss that prediction together. Then have the child read the next chapter to find out if the prediction is correct. Continue the activity until the book is finished. This activity can last for a few days if the book you choose has a lot of chapters.

Creating a Character

An imaginative child will enjoy becoming a favorite character for a day!

What You'll Need:

favorite book or story

costume props

Invite the child to choose a favorite character from a well-liked book. Help the child find descriptive passages in the book that tell about that character. Then invite the child to decide how that character would dress and act. For example, a very old lady might wear a shawl, use a hand-bag, and walk slowly while using a cane. Have a dress-up day when the child dresses up as the character of his or her choice and reads portions of the story aloud.

For further challenge, invite the child, while in character, to write a letter to another character from the story.

Mapping the Story

Mapping a story after reading it aids in understanding story structure.

What You'll Need:

book with several different settings

paper

pencil

crayons or markers

 Have the child read the book. Then ask the child to write down where the story begins and every location described in the book. Help the child make a colorful map of all the different places the book describes, labeling each location (school, someone's house, park, and so on). For an additional challenge, suggest the child add arrows showing the route the main character takes to go to these locations.

Peanut Butter Roll-Ups

Making these tasty, no-bake snacks is a great way for the child to practice following directions.

What You'll Need:

measuring spoons

mixing bowl

powdered sugar

powdered milk

peanut butter

pecan pieces

wooden spoon

tray or plate

Have the child follow these simple directions to make an easy, nutritious snack.

1. Put 2 tablespoons of powdered sugar in a mixing bowl.
2. Add 2 tablespoons of powdered milk.
3. Add 4 tablespoons of peanut butter.
4. Add ¼ cup pecan pieces.
5. Mix.
6. Roll the mixture into golf-ball-size circles, and place them on a tray or plate.
7. Put the roll-ups in the refrigerator for a few hours until cold.
8. Take out of the refrigerator and enjoy a tasty, nutritious snack.

If/Then Cards

Challenge the child's thinking skills with this game of cause-and-effect relationships.

What You'll Need:

Ten 3×5 index cards

scissors

markers

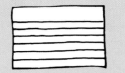

basket

 Cut ten index cards in half. On one half of each card write the word *IF*. Write the word *THEN* on the other half of each card. Give the child all the sets of cards. Invite the child to write or draw pictures on each card, using the if/then formula. Suggest using ideas from a familiar story or rhyme. You may wish to create one set of cards for the child as an example, such as:

"IF I jump in the puddle"

"THEN I will get wet"

To play the game, have the child scramble the cards. Challenge the child to match the top *if* half of a card with its corresponding *then* half to show a complete, reasonable idea.

Picture This!

The child takes on the role of a photographer while "taking pictures" of similar household objects.

What You'll Need:

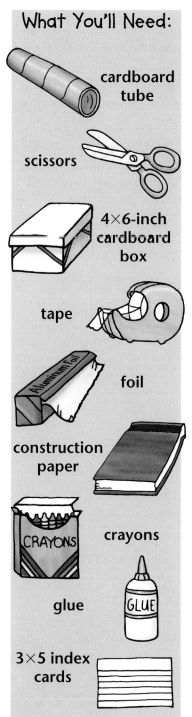

cardboard tube

scissors

4×6-inch cardboard box

tape

foil

construction paper

crayons

glue

3×5 index cards

Cut a 3½-inch ring from a cardboard tube. Cut four 1-inch slits around one end of the tube. Bend the slits out. Place the cardboard box on the table with the open side facing away from you. The open side is the back of the camera, and the bottom of the box is the front. Tape the tube to the bottom of the box (the front of the camera), with the slits flush against the box. Cover the box with foil, still leaving the back open. Draw shutters, lenses, and buttons on construction paper, cut them out, and glue them to the front and sides of the camera.

Next invite the child to "take photos" of pairs of household objects that are similar, such as objects that are the same shape. (The child can draw pictures on index cards and place them inside the camera.) At the end of the activity, remove the "photos" from the camera, and display them for others to see.

Shadow Play

The child will enjoy imaginative storytelling through these shadow puppets.

What You'll Need:

bright flashlight

Cast a bright light against a light-colored wall. Sit between the light and the wall, and demonstrate how to make shadow puppets by manipulating your hands to create the desired shadow images. For example, form a rabbit using your thumb to hold down the last two fingers on the same hand and having the pointer and middle fingers straight up, slightly apart.

Invite the child to use his or her imagination to create other shadow puppets on the wall. Then encourage the child to make up a story about these shadow characters and to perform the show for others.

Action Figures

Cartoon characters provide lots of opportunities to be exposed to common and proper nouns.

What You'll Need:

large piece of construction paper or posterboard

crayons or markers

Discuss the child's favorite cartoon and action characters from TV and the movies. Invite the child to draw these characters on a large piece of construction paper. Then have the child write the name of each character above the corresponding drawing. Below the drawing, have the child write what kind of creature the character is. While looking at the pictures, point out the differences between common nouns and proper nouns.

Don't Say What You See!

This picture-description activity challenges the child to find the right words to convey meaning.

What You'll Need:

3×5 index cards

crayons or markers

old magazines

scissors

clear tape or glue

shoe box

Create 15 to 20 picture cards of common animals or objects together. The cards can be simple drawings on index cards or pictures cut from old magazines and glued or taped onto the cards. Put the cards in a shoe box.

Invite the child to pull out a card and, without naming the animal or object, describe what is pictured. Make sure the child keeps the card hidden from your view. You are now allowed five chances to guess the name of the animal or object on the card. After the answer has been given, it is your turn to pick a card, describe what is pictured, and ask the child to guess its identity.

SIZE 5½

Blue Ribbon

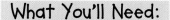

HIP, HIP, HOORAY! You'll be cheering, too, for the heroes in this rewarding activity about characters.

What You'll Need:

blue and yellow construction paper

scissors

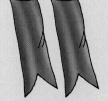

2 blue ribbon streamers

clear tape or glue

markers

FIRST PLACE! YOU'RE A WINNER! FUNNIEST DOG! HERO! YOU'RE NUMBER 1!

 Discuss different ways to describe a person or an animal that has accomplished an outstanding achievement. Then invite the child to design and create a blue-ribbon award for a favorite story character. Explain that the award may be for kindness, hard work, courage, or any other action or quality the child thinks is noteworthy. Create the ribbon from construction paper and blue ribbon streamers. Suggest that the child print the name of the character and the reason the award was given on the ribbon.

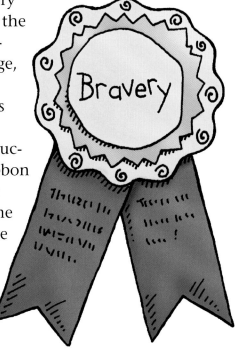

Weather Report

Amateur weather forecasters take over the weather reporting for the day in this adjective-based activity.

What You'll Need:

- paper
- pencil
- construction paper
- markers
- old magazines
- pointer

Allow the child to take on the role of weather forecaster for the day. As he or she prepares to report the weather, have the child make a list of adjectives describing different weather conditions, such as *sunny, rainy, windy, cloudy, snowy, hot, cold,* and so on. Use the construction paper to make props, such as pictures to represent the weather symbols, maps, and photographs. Also look through old magazines for weather pictures you can use. Encourage the young forecaster to use a pointer with the props to make the presentation more visual.

Review verbs by having the child name activities he or she likes to do on sunny, snowy, rainy, or windy days.

Report Cards

Make a mock report card to see if characters in favorite stories and books make the grade.

What You'll Need:

construction paper

felt-tip pen

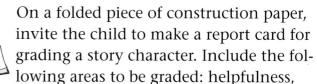

On a folded piece of construction paper, invite the child to make a report card for grading a story character. Include the following areas to be graded: helpfulness, attitude, sense of humor, completing assignments, following rules, and being on time. The report card is not complete until the child "grades" the character in each of the selected areas. The child may even find it necessary to request a conference with the character's parents. If so, this should be noted on the report card, too.

Bookmarks

These decorative bookmarks will help the child keep his or her place when reading a favorite book.

What You'll Need:

favorite book

card stock

scissors

felt-tip pen

markers

Have the child read a favorite book. Then cut the card stock into the size of a bookmark (roughly 2×8 inches). Explain to the child that a bookmark not only marks a page but can also be used to summarize the book. Invite the child to summarize the book on the bookmark. Remind the child to choose words carefully so they fit in the small area. Once the summary has been written on the bookmark, invite the child to decorate it with markers.

Funny, Foolish, False

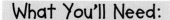

This statement-making activity enhances the child's understanding of the way language can be used.

What You'll Need:

strips of paper

pencil

small paper bag

 Write words that describe different kinds of statements on strips of paper. These descriptions can include words such as *funny, silly, foolish, true, exaggerated, false,* and *wise.* Discuss with the child the meaning of these words, and then put the strips of paper into a small paper bag. Pick a piece of paper from the bag, and make a statement that can be identified or labeled by the word written on the card. For example, if you pull out a strip of paper with the word *silly* written on it, you might say, "Bears wear shoes." Next, invite the child to do the same thing. Take turns pulling pieces of paper out of the bag until all the words have been chosen.

Face It!

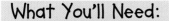

Get ready to "Face It!" as the child explores character expressions.

What You'll Need:

old magazines

scissors

colored construction paper

clear tape or glue

crayons or markers

 Invite the child to cut out pictures of faces from old magazines. The faces the child chooses should show specific expressions, such as happy, sad, angry, scared, excited, worried, or surprised. Have the child glue or tape the expressive faces on colored construction paper. Then invite the child to add speech or thought balloons with words the child thinks the people are saying or thinking.

I LOVE ICE CREAM!

To take this one step further, have the child glue two or three faces onto one sheet of construction paper and create a cartoon conversation between them.

Chow Down

Explore a character's likes and dislikes in this activity that's sure to make you hungry.

What You'll Need:

favorite books

old magazines

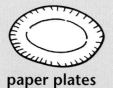

scissors

paper plates

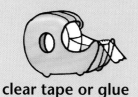

clear tape or glue

 Have the child look through a collection of favorite books and select one with a main character he or she is particularly fond of. Invite the child to explain why he or she likes the character. Then help the child plan a meal for that character. Start by cutting out pictures of various foods from old magazines. Then tape or glue the pictures to a paper plate to show what will be served. If the character is an animal, help the child research the kind of food that animal eats. The child may also wish to create a just-for-fun menu that is sure to whet his or her favorite character's appetite.

Event Hangers

Understanding cause-and-effect relationships in reading is made simple with this creative activity.

What You'll Need:

- clothes hangers
- paper
- clear tape or glue
- favorite story
- markers
- old magazines
- scissors
- tagboard
- hole punch
- yarn

Cover the hole in a hanger (but don't wrap the hook!) with blank paper. Use tape or glue to hold the paper firmly in place. Set the hanger aside for now.

Begin by having the child read a favorite story. Then invite the child to draw a picture on the paper-covered hanger that shows an important event in the story. Next have the child draw pictures or cut out pictures from old magazines that show what caused the event to happen. Glue or tape the pictures on tagboard cutouts. Help the child punch a hole in the top of each tagboard shape and in the bottom of the paper-covered hanger. String yarn through the holes, tie, and hang the cutouts from the clothes hanger. Put the hanger on display so others may see it.

As a variation, have the child draw or find pictures to illustrate what happened before and after the event pictured on the hanger and attach them as well.

Snowy Day Fun

Warm up a snowy day with this activity by finding various ways to have fun in the snow.

What You'll Need:

a book or story featuring snow

dark paper

pencil

white glue

scissors

construction paper

Read the book or story aloud together. Discuss all kinds of ways to have fun in snow. One way is to make a snowman. Help the child make a snowman on paper by drawing the outline of a snowman on dark paper with a pencil. Fill in the outline with white glue. Allow the glue to dry. Cut various items from construction paper, such as a hat, a broom, and gloves, and glue those in place. You may want to create a whole snow family on the paper. Label them with names, by role, or by other characteristics.

Poem Pictures

Capture with colors the pictures that poems paint with words!

What You'll Need:

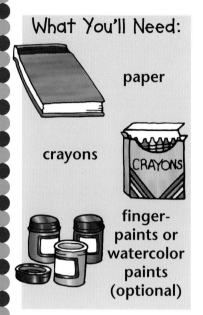

paper

crayons

finger-paints or watercolor paints (optional)

 Share a favorite poem with the child. Invite the child to describe what and who the poem is about and the scene where it might take place. The child can then draw a picture to illustrate the poem as imagined. For a variation, the child can create different illustrations for the poem (or for other poems) using different media, such as fingerpaints or watercolors.

Story Hanger

Door hangers are not only for clothes! They can also be used to tell about a favorite storybook.

What You'll Need:

tagboard

pencil

scissors

felt-tip pens

 Draw and cut a door hanger out of tagboard. Be sure to make it large enough to fit on a doorknob. Then encourage the child to write the title and author of a favorite book or story on the back of the hanger. He or she can then draw a picture or write a sentence about the book on the front of the tagboard hanger.

Invite the child to place the hanger on a friend or sibling's door, desk, or coat hook to encourage them to read the book, too.

Hero Poster

Making posters is a creative activity that encourages reading and writing.

What You'll Need:

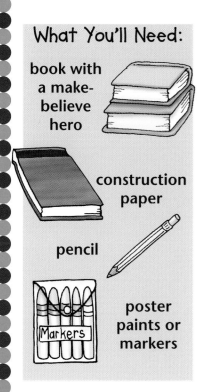

book with a make-believe hero

construction paper

pencil

poster paints or markers

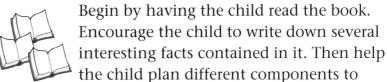

Begin by having the child read the book. Encourage the child to write down several interesting facts contained in it. Then help the child plan different components to include in a promotional poster for the hero of the book. For example, the poster might feature famous moments, heroic qualities, challenges the hero faced, photographs or drawings of the hero, and so forth. Be ready for some poster-creating fun!

Character Comparisons

Compare and contrast characters who live in different stories.

What You'll Need:

2 stories

After reading two different stories, invite the child to talk about the main characters from each of them. Encourage the child to describe ways in which the people or animals were similar and ways in which they were different. The child can also talk about how their situations, their problems, their families, where they lived, or what they liked to eat were similar or different. For a more challenging activity, the child can imagine and describe what each character might have done if they were placed into the middle of the other character's story!

Character Mobile

The child will become familiar with characters in a favorite story when creating a character mobile.

What You'll Need:

favorite book or story

paper

markers

tagboard

scissors

clear tape or glue

hole punch

10- to 12-inch polystyrene plate

yarn

 Begin by inviting the child to draw and label pictures of various characters from a favorite story. Cut out different shapes (squares, circles, triangles) from the tagboard, and have the child mount each picture on individual tagboard shapes using glue. Punch one hole in the top of each shape and enough holes around the outside edge of a polystyrene plate for each of the shapes. Have the child thread yarn strands through the shapes and plates and then tie the yarn so the shapes dangle from the plate. Hang the finished mobile in a room for all to see.

To take this activity further, the child can add a word to each label describing a trait that character has.

Chapter 2
Alphabet Adventures

Picture Dictionary

This dictionary provides the child with a powerful tool for alphabetizing, spelling, and learning new words.

What You'll Need:

clear tape

several 18×6-inch strips of construction paper

markers

 Invite the child to make a picture dictionary of new spelling words. Choose the words from a school spelling list or from words the child wants to learn to spell. Help the child tape the 18×6-inch strips of paper together, end to end. Fold the long strip back and forth, accordion-style, creating about three sections to each 18-inch strip. Make sure there are 26 pages and a cover. Then have the child decorate the book cover.

Next, the child should write one letter of the alphabet, from *Aa* to *Zz*, on each page. The child can then write the spelling words on the appropriate page. You may want to help the child alphabetize the words before they are written in the picture dictionary. Finally, help the child write a definition and draw a colorful illustration for each entry.

Express Mail

Writing, mailing, and delivering these special phonics letters will keep the young mail carrier's hands full.

What You'll Need:

3 shoe boxes with lids

scissors

crayons

3×5 index cards

envelopes

Cut a 4$\frac{1}{2}$-inch slit in the lid of each shoe box. Write a letter (or cluster of letters, such as *d, t, str,* or *m*) on the front of each box. Invite the child to pretend to be a mail carrier whose job is to sort and deliver the mail. With crayons, have the child draw pictures of objects that begin with each of the letters on the mailboxes on several 3×5 index cards. Then have the child place each picture in an envelope, address the envelopes, and deliver them to the correct mailbox.

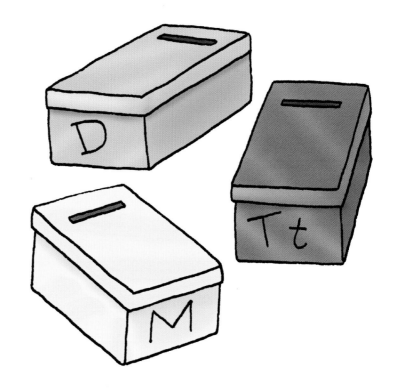

Dear Wise Owl

Invite the child to get to the bottom of this puzzling letter about a mysterious box.

What You'll Need:

large piece of construction paper

markers

notebook paper

pen or pencil

Read the following letter to the child:

Dear Wise Owl,
When I opened the front door this morning, there was a large box on my doorstep. It was wrapped in shiny red paper and had a giant bow. Just as I was about to open the box, it moved! What do you think is in the box? What should I do with it?
Please tell me what you think!
Brandon

Have the child write the letters of the alphabet down the left side of a large piece of construction paper. Ask him or her to suggest creative ideas for what may be in the box. Invite the child to think of a word that begins with each letter, or as many of the letters as he or she can, and to write each word on the

construction paper next to the appropriate letter. Have the child decide on one item from the list that he or she thinks is most likely inside the box. Then help the child write a response to Brandon, telling him what he or she thinks is in the box and what Brandon should do.

Break the Code

The child becomes a spelling sleuth while trying to break secret codes.

What You'll Need:

paper

felt-tip pen

pencil

Help the child make a code breaker. Begin by drawing a wheel pattern, like the one shown here, with a felt-tip pen. Write the letters of the alphabet in sequential order in the spaces on the outer edge of the larger wheel, and write their corresponding numbers, 1–26, on the inner wheel as shown.

Next, spin the wheel to determine a code. Write a secret message on a separate piece of paper in code; that is, substitute the corresponding number for each letter. Then the child can take on the role of a young sleuth and decode a secret message by using the code breaker. For example, a message in code might read:

13-5-5-20 13-5 1-20 20-8-5 6-15-18-20!

Using the decoder, the child could easily spell out the real words:

M-E-E-T M-E A-T T-H-E F-O-R-T!

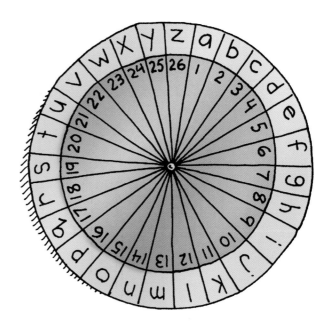

Stretch-a-Word

In this activity the child exercises the body and the mind for the sake of spelling.

What You'll Need:

nine 11×17-inch pieces of colored construction paper

masking tape

markers

 Tape nine pieces of colored paper on the floor to make a 3×3 grid large enough for the child to stretch out on. Write the letters *a, b, d, f, m, n, p, s,* and *t* in the construction-paper squares of the grid. The letter *a* should be in the middle.

To play the game, say a three-letter word that has the short vowel *a* sound, such as *fan* or *nap*. Have the child spell the word by putting his or her feet on the first letter, the left hand on the second letter (which will always be *a*), and the right hand on the third letter.

For a more challenging game, have the child spell four- or five-letter words, using both hands, both feet, and even his or her head!

Taco Surprise

Learning about nouns was never as much fun as it is in this taco surprise!

What You'll Need:

paper

pen or pencil

taco ingredients

cooking utensils

plates

napkins

 Help the child learn about nouns as you make tacos together. Begin by listing the materials you will need. Then have the child divide the materials into three noun groups: ingredients, cooking utensils, and serving materials. Using these lists as guides, carefully gather the necessary materials, and set them out on a table or other large work area. Take care to prepare the ingredients before you begin. To make the tacos, follow this simple recipe, adapting it to personal taste.

1. Fully cook beef or chicken, drain, and set aside.

2. Heat taco shells in warm oven for 3–5 minutes.

3. Spoon meat into bottom of heated taco shell.

4. Top with shredded lettuce, chopped tomatoes, chopped green peppers, sliced olives, shredded cheese, taco sauce, and sour cream.

5. Serve and eat!

INGREDIENTS	COOKING UTENSILS	SERVING MATERIALS
sour cream	spoon	plates
lettuce	knife	napkins
tomato	cookie sheet	
green pepper	oven	
beef	pot holders	
chicken		
olives		
cheese		
taco sauce		
taco shells		

Diamond Poem

While composing this poem about a favorite pet, the child will use words that are real gems!

What You'll Need:

posterboard

markers

 Invite the child to write a poem in the shape of a diamond about a favorite pet. Help the child write the poem by following these line-by-line instructions and writing the words described.

Line 1—Kind of pet

Line 2—Two adjectives that describe the pet's shape or size

Line 3—Three verbs that end with *ing* and tell what the pet does

Line 4—Four nouns that name what the pet likes

Line 5—Three verbs that end with *ing* and tell what the pet does, different than those in Line 3

Line 6—Two adjectives that describe the pet's personality

Line 7—Name of the pet

Invite the child to share the poem with you. Then look at the poem again with the child, pointing out the nouns. Look again for verbs, and then for adjectives. You should find an abundance of each.

Hamster
tiny, chubby,
hiding, running, chewing,
carrots, lettuce, apples, oats,
gnawing, nibbling, squeaking,
sweet, shy
Furball

Yak-a-Sak!

Creating new sentences from random sentence parts is a hilarious way to practice building sentences.

What You'll Need:

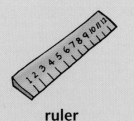

paper

ruler

scissors

pen or pencil

2 paper bags

 Sentences are made up of two basic parts: the subject, or naming part (for example, *red, juicy tomatoes*) and the predicate, or telling part (*are growing in the garden*).

For this activity, invite the child to think of ten simple sentences and write each of them on a separate strip of paper. Cut the strips of paper between the naming parts and the telling parts so that each sentence is cut in two pieces. Label two paper bags as shown. Place all of the naming parts in the correct bag, and place all of the telling parts in the other bag. Next, have the child pick one sentence part from each sack and combine them to make a sentence. Prepare yourself for some silly sentences.

For additional creative fun, invite the child to illustrate the silly sentences with pencils or crayons.

Cookie Cutter Words

Here's a tasty way for the child to practice spelling theme-related words.

What You'll Need:

prepared sugar cookie dough

flour

knife

cookie sheet

edible sprinkles

spatula

waxed paper or paper plate

Set out prepared cookie dough on a surface covered with flour (so the dough doesn't stick) while discussing words related to a particular theme. Carefully cut the dough into letters. Have the child spell these theme-related words by arranging the cookie-dough letters on a cookie sheet. Invite the child to decorate the cookies with sprinkles before you bake them in the oven. Once the cookies have cooled, remove them from the cookie sheet with the spatula, and place them on waxed paper or a paper plate. Review the spelling of each word with the child before enjoying the tasty spelling treat.

Mix 'n' Match Letters

Encourage young artists to create this collage of letters while learning new spelling words.

What You'll Need:

old magazines and newspapers

scissors

clear tape or glue

wallpaper

Discuss words with the child related to a current social studies or science theme. Then gather some old magazines and newspapers to look at. Have the child point to individual letters that are needed to spell each theme-related word. Next cut out the letters the child has indicated. Help the child tape or glue the letters to spell out the theme-related words on sheets of patterned wallpaper to make creative theme collages.

Spelling Volcano

Engage the child in this challenging activity of wits and vocabulary.

What You'll Need:

pen or pencil

paper

 Begin by drawing a set of boxes in the shape of a volcano, like the example shown here: two boxes at the top, followed by a row of three boxes, a row of four boxes, a row of five boxes, and so on up to seven. Then write a two-letter word on the top row. Have the child add one new letter to that word to spell a new word. The new letter can be added to the beginning, middle, or end of the two-letter word. Write the new word in the second row of the volcano. Continue in this way, adding one new letter at each row to make a new word, going as far down the volcano as possible. Can the child make it to the bottom with a seven-letter word?

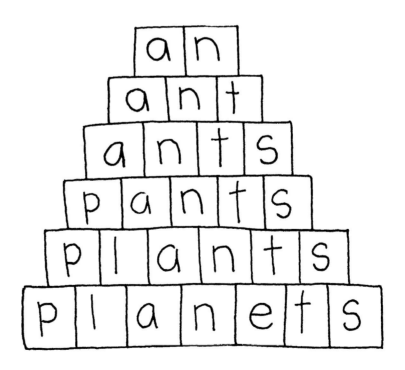

Past Tense Sense

The child will identify and use past tense verbs while creating a decorative scrapbook page!

What You'll Need:

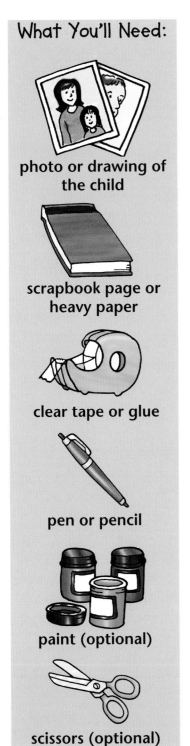

photo or drawing of the child

scrapbook page or heavy paper

clear tape or glue

pen or pencil

paint (optional)

scissors (optional)

Find a photograph of the child, or have the child draw his or her own picture. Have the child tape or glue the picture or drawing on a piece of paper. Encourage the child to decorate the page using one or more of the following suggestions: paint a border, glue or tape a paper frame around the picture, use fancy letters to write a caption, add ticket stubs or other souvenirs associated with the picture. Invite the child to write a sentence at the bottom of the scrapbook page to tell what the picture is about. Remind the child to write in the past tense.

I skied down Sugar Mountain.

Letter Collages

Cut it, glue it, paste it! This creative activity is sure to keep hands busy.

What You'll Need:

ABC books

heavy paper (precut into large letters)

old magazines

scissors

clear tape or glue

hole punch

string

Read aloud a variety of ABC books with the child. Point out the pictures, the letters, and the corresponding beginning sounds as you read. Next give the child large paper letters that you have cut out in advance. Ask the child to cut out pictures from old magazines of objects that begin with the sound each letter stands for—for example, a cat and a car for the letter *c*, and a dog, a deer, and a door for the letter *d*. Encourage the child to cover the entire letter with the pictures to create a colorful letter collage. To complete the project, punch a hole in the top of each letter, and hang it in a room.

Just for the Taste of It!

The child will eat adjectives with this tasty activity.

What You'll Need:

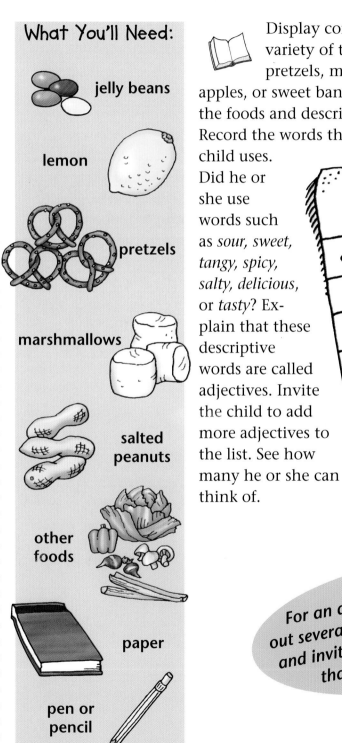

jelly beans

lemon

pretzels

marshmallows

salted peanuts

other foods

paper

pen or pencil

Display common foods that include a wide variety of tastes, such as jelly beans, lemons, pretzels, marshmallows, peanuts, raisins, sour apples, or sweet banana peppers. Let the child sample the foods and describe how they taste. Record the words the child uses. Did he or she use words such as *sour, sweet, tangy, spicy, salty, delicious,* or *tasty*? Explain that these descriptive words are called adjectives. Invite the child to add more adjectives to the list. See how many he or she can think of.

> sour
> lemon
> salty
> peanuts
> sweet
> jelly beans

For an additional challenge, set out several foods with strong aromas and invite the child to record words that capture their smells.

Pasta Pizzazz

This entertaining spelling project allows the child to analyze spelling patterns while creating wearable art.

What You'll Need:

rigatoni noodles (without ridges if possible)

paints

paintbrush

felt-tip pen

strands of yarn

Have the child paint uncooked rigatoni noodles. Once the paint is dry, ask the child to write the following words on the noodles: *hen, pen, Ben*. String the noodles on a piece of yarn. Do the same for this next batch of words: *cake, wake, take*.

Next, ask the child to look at the words on each strand, identify the spelling pattern (in this case *en* and *ake*), and make new word noodles to add to each. Help the child tie the finished strands to create wearable spelling art.

For a challenging variation, invite the child to construct a sentence using as many words from the wearable art as possible. Expect some silly sentences!

20 Seconds

The spotlight is on verb tenses in this memory-teasing activity.

What You'll Need:

**several small items
(buttons, pens,
beads, spools of
thread, etc.)**

tray

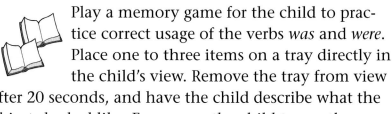 Play a memory game for the child to practice correct usage of the verbs *was* and *were*. Place one to three items on a tray directly in the child's view. Remove the tray from view after 20 seconds, and have the child describe what the objects looked like. Encourage the child to use the words *was* or *were* in the sentence.

Jumpin' Jimminy

The child will practice spelling words frequently used in reading and writing while jumping from X to X.

What You'll Need:

masking tape

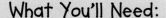

list of spelling words

Place masking tape *X*s in a path around the room. Have the child stand behind the first *X*. Explain that the object of this game is to jump from one *X* to another until the child reaches the end of the path. Begin by reading words for the child to spell, focusing on words the child uses frequently. Some examples may include: *the, come,* and *said*. For a correctly spelled word, the child jumps ahead one *X*. The child does not move if he or she has spelled the word incorrectly. As the child jumps forward, start reading harder words, possibly words from a school spelling list. For spelling especially difficult words correctly, you may offer the child two jumps ahead. So get ready, get set, spell, and jump!

For an interesting twist, have the child use each spelling word correctly in a sentence.

Waldorf Salad

The child will enjoy learning about verbs while you chop, slice, and mix a Waldorf salad.

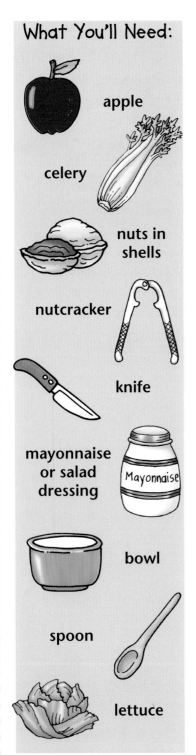

What You'll Need:

apple

celery

nuts in shells

nutcracker

knife

mayonnaise or salad dressing

Mayonnaise

bowl

spoon

lettuce

Set out an apple, a stalk of celery, and some nuts. Ask the child to use simple words to explain what someone might do to each of the foods before eating them. Make a list of the action verbs suggested by the child. Then carefully prepare the ingredients according to the following recipe for a Waldorf salad. (When you chop up the ingredients, be sure to remind the child that he or she should always be very careful around knives.)

Mix together:
—1 chopped apple
—1 sliced celery stalk
—½ cup chopped nuts
—½ cup mayonnaise or salad dressing
Serve on a bed of lettuce.

wash
peel
cut
chop

Web Words

This chip-flipping activity provides lots of practice for spelling words with the short e sound.

What You'll Need:

posterboard

markers

flat plastic chips

Before beginning, help the child draw a large web on a piece of posterboard like the one shown here. In each section of the web, have the child draw a picture of an object pronounced with a short *e*, as in *web*.

To play the game, set two chips on a hard surface, such as a table or tile floor, next to the web game board. Instruct the child to bounce the chip off the surface to make it "jump" or "flip" into the air and then land on the web. The child may want to take a few practice flips. Then have the child say and spell the name of the picture that the chip has landed on. Continue until the child has spelled all the pictures.

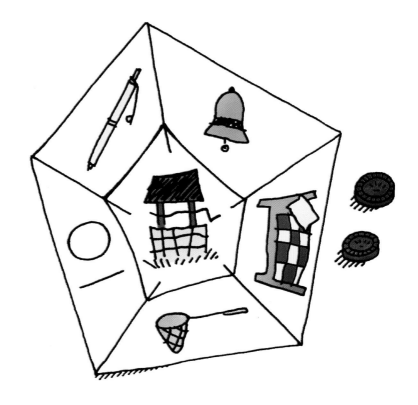

Cheer 'Em Up!

Try this combination of markers and glitter to create a colorful, cheerful greeting.

What You'll Need:

8×10-inch posterboard, folded in half

felt-tip pens

glitter

glue

markers

Invite the child to create a cheerful greeting card. Begin by having the child write a greeting on the front of the card in large, decorative letters. Then have the child write a short note to the recipient on the inside of the folded card. Next, set out glitter, glue, and colored markers, and encourage the child to decorate the card with a little color and sparkle. When the card is dry, it is ready to be given to that special someone who needs some cheer!

Vested Interest

This activity will give the child a vested interest in beginning letters and sounds.

What You'll Need:

paper bag

scissors

paint

paintbrushes

old magazines

clear tape or glue

 Turn a large paper bag upside down, and cut it straight up the middle. Make a neck opening by cutting an oval shape in the top (formerly bottom) of the bag. Make armholes by cutting circles in the sides of the bag. Invite the child to choose a letter of the alphabet to paint on the newly created vest. Then suggest the child look through old magazines to find pictures of objects that begin with that letter, cut them out, and tape or glue them to the vest.

Fuzzy, Bristly Words

The child may feel itchy or bumpy all in the name of learning adjectives.

What You'll Need:

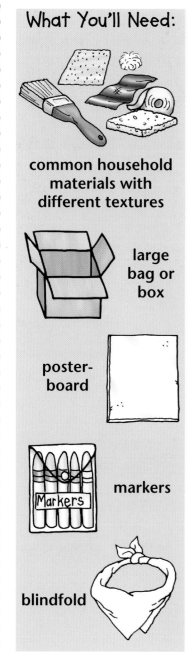

common household materials with different textures

large bag or box

poster-board

markers

blindfold

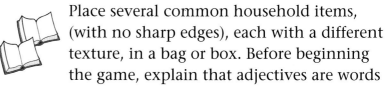 Place several common household items, (with no sharp edges), each with a different texture, in a bag or box. Before beginning the game, explain that adjectives are words that describe nouns. Then draw a word web (see page 55) and write the sentence "It feels _____." in the center. Blindfold the child, and instruct him or her to place one hand inside the bag or box. Ask the child to describe what the objects feel like. Write the words the child uses on the web. Can the child guess what objects are in the bag?

To add a new angle to this activity, put several pairs of textured objects in the bag or box. Invite the blindfolded child to grab an object, describe how it feels, and then, only by touching, find its match.

Pudding Play

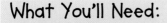

Finger painting was never as much fun as it is with this pudding project. And cleanup is as easy as 1–2–3!

What You'll Need:

premixed pudding

sponge

dishpan

Begin by pouring a cup of premixed pudding on a clean, flat work surface. Invite the child to spread it around with his or her fingers. Then review final consonants by saying a word and having the child write the whole word or just the final letter in the pudding. The child can "erase" the word or letter by rubbing over it with his or her fingertips. Continue by having the child write and erase final consonants for as long as the pudding lasts. Pudding inevitably gets licked off fingers and out of the bowl during this activity, so it will not last too long. For easy cleanup, set out a sponge and a dishpan filled with soapy water.

Chapter 3
Celebrating Stories

Finger Puppets

Make puppets from old gloves, and create a cast of actors for dramatic discussion and interaction!

What You'll Need:

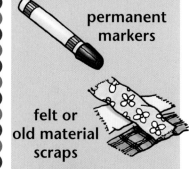

old gloves or rubber dishwashing gloves

permanent markers

felt or old material scraps

yarn

glue

scissors

This activity gives the child creative freedom to express thoughts and ideas through puppetry. It also provides an opportunity for the child to extend imaginative and emotional responses through language.

Begin by helping the child make faces on the fingers of old gloves or rubber dishwashing gloves. For rubber dishwashing gloves, draw faces with permanent markers; for cloth gloves, glue small pieces of felt, yarn, or cloth scraps for faces. Carefully cut the fingers off the gloves. The child will now have finished finger puppets that can talk, sing, discuss, or whisper at the child's discretion.

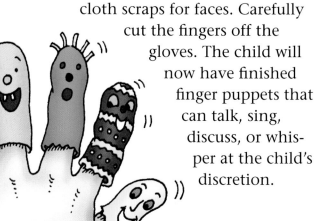

Museum Display

Here's an activity that lets the child create a mini-museum while learning about nouns.

What You'll Need:

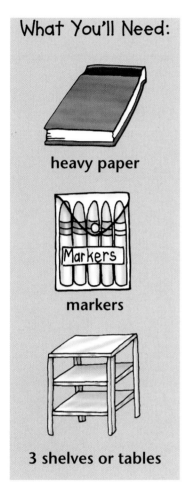

heavy paper

markers

3 shelves or tables

Discuss the art, science, or history museums you or the child have visited in the past and the kinds of things you each saw there. Also explain to the child that a noun is a word that names a person, place, or thing. Then help the child create a museum display of nouns by labeling exhibit areas as "People," "Places," and "Things." You may want to use empty shelves in a bookcase as your display area. Other good display areas include windowsills, cardboard boxes, and tabletops.

Next have the child arrange collections of appropriate objects, such as stuffed animals and pictures, for each shelf in the display. It might be fun to set museum tour hours and then invite family members or friends to visit the museum. The child may want to act as a museum tour guide during the visits. Tell the child that a tour guide is someone who explains the exhibits to the visitors and answers their questions.

Story Pizza

Slice, mix, sort, and arrange pieces of a story as you create a delicious story pizza.

What You'll Need:

cardboard

scissors

pie pan

markers

Cut a circle in the cardboard the same diameter as the pie pan. Pretend that the circle is a large pizza. Invite the child to imagine what toppings the pizza would have on it and how it would look, smell, and taste. Then cut the cardboard pie into three equal slices. Discuss with the child events at the beginning, the middle, and the end of a favorite story. Have the child draw a picture or write at least one sentence that tells about an event in the story on a separate piece of pizza. Then have the child put the slices of pizza in the pie pan in the correct order, working clockwise, while retelling the story.

Cut new story pizzas into more and more slices—four, six, or eight—and have the child list events in more detail on each slice.

Category Challenge

You'll need to sharpen your pencil and your wits for this word-category game.

What You'll Need:

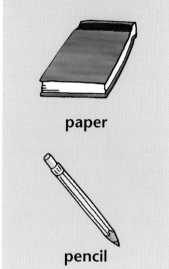

paper

pencil

Have the child draw a grid on a piece of paper, six squares across and four squares down. Next, choose four consonants and one vowel together, and write them in boxes two through six across the top. Think of categories, and list them down the left side. Start with only a few categories, and add more as the child gets used to the game. The object is to come up with a word that begins with each letter in the top row and is part of the category listed on the side. Invite the child to fill in and complete the game board within a designated time period (3–10 minutes).

	B	G	S	R	A
ANIMAL	bear	goat	snake	rat	ape
FOOD	banana		soup	radish	apple

Flip, Flap, Flop

The child will flip while uncovering directions in sequence!

What You'll Need:

12×18-inch piece of paper folded in half lengthwise

scissors

crayons or markers

 Invite the child to describe steps in a familiar process, such as preparing a bowl of cereal, building a wooden block castle, or brushing teeth. Help the child cut three or more flaps in the top half of the paper, depending on the number of steps in the process. (There should be one flap for each step.) Cut from the edge of the paper toward the fold. Then have the child write the steps on the underside of the sheet, with one step underneath each flap. Write the corresponding numeral (*1, 2, 3*) on the covering flap to show the order of the steps. Have the child turn up each flap as he or she describes the sequence.

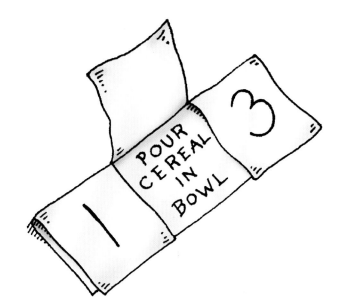

Pop-Up Publishing

Bring books to life with pop-up people and more.

What You'll Need:

paper

scissors

crayons

glue

 The child can help make a pop-up book by creating the pop-up pictures and inventing the story! To make the pop-up pages for the book, fold a piece of paper in half. Then cut two 1½-inch-long slits approximately 1½ inches apart in the middle of the folded edge of the paper. Push the cut area (the paper between the two cuts) to the inside of the fold in order to form a pop-up section. The child can draw a picture for the pop-up on another piece of paper, cut it out, and glue it onto the pop-up section. The child can then draw the background on the original pop-up page. Depending on the length of the story the child makes up, it can be contained within one pop-up page, or several pages can be pasted together to make a pop-up book.

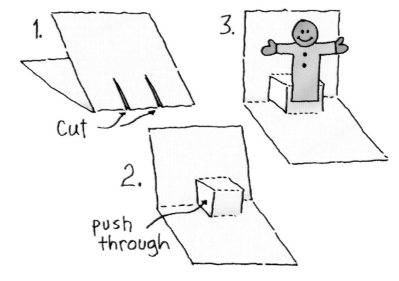

1. Cut

2. push through

3.

Shared Word Stories

Combine groups of unrelated words to spur story narration. Expect some creative results.

What You'll Need:

pencil

paper

Begin by writing five words on a sheet of paper. Invite the child to do the same on another piece of paper. Then, by using the words from both your list and the child's list, take turns making up and reciting a short story that includes all ten words.

Make It Modern

In this creative retelling activity, the child brings favorite characters to life in modern times.

Invite the child to retell a familiar folk or fairy tale, such as "The Three Little Pigs" or "Cinderella," but to change the setting to the place where you live and to modern times. If the story took place today, for example, what would be the same? What would be different? If the three little pigs were building their house next door, what materials would they use? Who would they ask for supplies? Would they call each other on cell phones when the wolf was blowing down their houses? If Cinderella lived in your town, where would she live? Where would the prince live? What would she wear to the ball?

Hat Parade

A hodgepodge of hats opens the door to delightful drama!

What You'll Need:

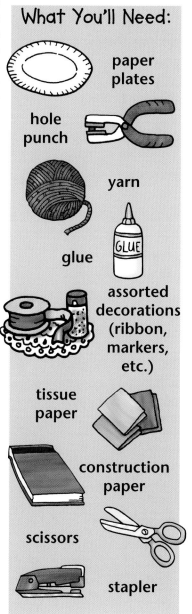

paper plates

hole punch

yarn

glue

assorted decorations (ribbon, markers, etc.)

tissue paper

construction paper

scissors

stapler

 With adult help, the child can make an assortment of hats and then use them to invent stories and for other dramatic play.

Paper Plate Hat: Use a hole punch to punch a hole on both sides of a paper plate. Thread and tie a piece of thick yarn through each hole. The child can decorate the top of the hat by gluing on ribbons, tissue paper, and strips of construction paper. When the hat is completed, the yarn strips can be tied to hold the hat on the child's head. For a variation, cut a large hole in the middle of the paper plate so that the hat is a brim only, and invite the child to decorate the brim.

Band and Strip Hat: Use a thick strip of construction paper to make a band that fits around the child's head. Staple the ends of the band together. The child can use additional strips of construction paper to make the crown of the hat by stapling them in arches from one side of the band to the other. The child can glue on decorations or use markers to color on the strips and arches.

Cylinder Hat: Bend a large piece of construction paper into a cylinder to fit on the child's head. The child can cut slits (approximately 1½ inches long) all around the bottom edge and then bend the cut paper out. Cut a hole the size of the cylinder in the middle of a paper plate, then let the child slide the plate over the top of the cylinder to where the slits begin. The child can glue the slits to the bottom of the plate to create a brim. The child can then decorate the hat.

Hung Out to Dry

Come join the three little kittens in their search for sentence order.

What You'll Need:

large index cards

pen or pencil

clothesline and clothespins

 Read or chant the familiar nursery rhyme "Three Little Kittens" with the child.

Three little kittens, they lost their mittens,
And they began to cry,
"Oh, mother dear, we sadly fear
That we have lost our mittens."
"What! lost your mittens, you naughty kittens!
Then you shall have no pie.
Mee-ow, mee-ow, mee-ow.
No, you shall have no pie."

Choose one or two sentences from the rhyme. Write each word of the sentence or sentences on individual cards, and mix up the cards. Then have the child arrange and hang the cards on the clothesline in sequential order to make complete sentences.

Magnetic Melodrama

Use magnets to keep paper actors on the move!

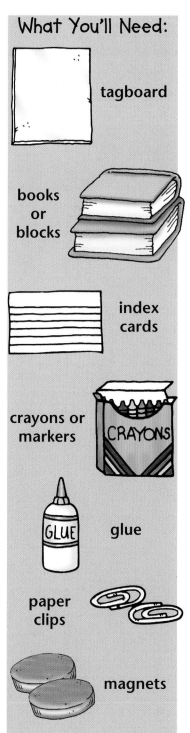

What You'll Need:

tagboard

books or blocks

index cards

crayons or markers

CRAYONS

glue

paper clips

magnets

 The child can create a stage for paper actors by setting a piece of tagboard across two stacks of blocks or books. Next, the child can make the "actors" by folding back the bottom third of an index card and drawing a picture of a person, an animal, or an imaginary creature on the top portion. The child should then glue a paper clip to the bottom of the folded-back portion. When the glue is dry, the child can place all the actors on the stage and start making up stories about them. To enhance the storytelling, the child can pull a magnet underneath the tagboard stage to move the characters around.

For a melodramatic magnet variation, the child can make refrigerator magnet faces! You can find round magnets (approximately 1 inch across) at a hardware or hobby store. Cut circles the same size as the magnets out of tagboard or other stiff paper. The child can draw faces on the stiff paper with markers and then glue the faces to the magnets.

Sports Heroes

This creative reading and recording activity is for sports fans of all ages.

What You'll Need:

book about a favorite sports figure

newspapers or magazines with information about that person

notebook

pencil

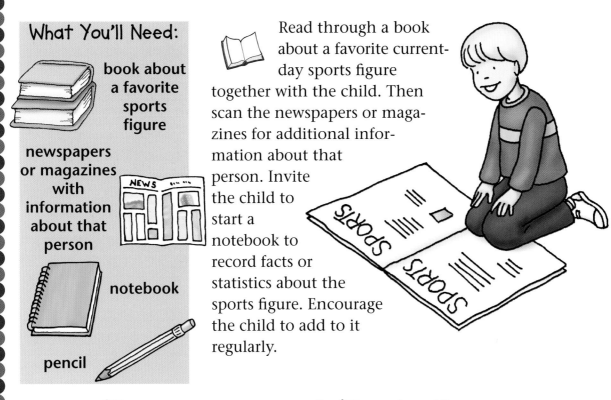

Read through a book about a favorite current-day sports figure together with the child. Then scan the newspapers or magazines for additional information about that person. Invite the child to start a notebook to record facts or statistics about the sports figure. Encourage the child to add to it regularly.

Rearranged Retellings

Here is a wacky way for the child to communicate information in sequence.

What You'll Need:

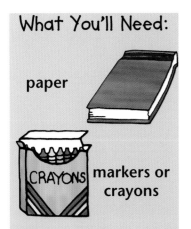

paper

markers or crayons

Help the child draw four or five separate pictures depicting four or five major events of a traditional or favorite story. Have the child lay out the pictures in sequential order and tell the story. Then randomly rearrange the pictures, and challenge the child to make up and tell a new version of the story in which the events occur in the new order. Expect some hilarious results!

Mask Making

Take part in making masks, then masquerade while play acting!

What You'll Need:

- large paper bags
- markers or crayons
- scissors
- glue
- construction paper
- fabric scraps
- yarn
- ribbon

Turn large paper bags into masks! Place the paper bag over the child's head, and carefully mark holes for the eyes. Remove the bag, and cut the holes or invite the child to cut them. Recheck the eyeholes for good visibility, and adjust them for the child's best viewing. The child can then decorate the bag by coloring it or gluing on pieces of construction paper, fabric scraps, yarn, and ribbon. Fabric scraps or paper can be used to create animal ears, and the ribbon and yarn can be glued on the top of the bag to create hair.

For a simpler mask, cut eyeholes in a paper plate and decorate it. Glue a strip of cardboard to the bottom of the plate to use as a handle to hold the mask.

Magazine Picture Puppets

These simple puppets offer an easy way to engage the child in language expression and development.

What You'll Need:

old magazines

cardboard

scissors

glue

craft sticks

Begin by helping the child cut out pictures of people and animals from old magazines. Glue the pictures to cardboard for sturdy backing, and cut around the picture shape. Next, glue a craft stick to the back of the cardboard. The craft stick will be the puppet's handle. When the glue on the picture puppets is dry, the child can use them to act out and tell made-up stories.

Felt Board Backdrops

The child's sequencing skills will be enhanced through this creative storytelling activity.

What You'll Need:

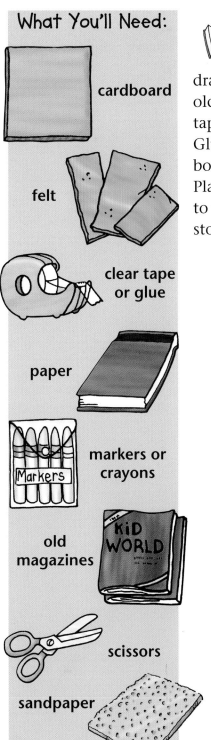

cardboard

felt

clear tape or glue

paper

markers or crayons

old magazines

scissors

sandpaper

Help the child make a felt board by gluing or taping a large piece of felt or felt squares onto a large piece of cardboard. Invite the child to draw or to cut out pictures of people and animals from old magazines. Then make those pictures sturdy by taping or gluing them onto small pieces of cardboard. Glue a small piece of sandpaper to the back of the cardboard so the story piece will stick to the felt board. Place the pictures on the felt board, and invite the child to use the characters to dramatize and tell a made-up story or to retell a favorite one.

Word Sort

This sorting activity is a creative way of putting information in order, a skill necessary for reading.

What You'll Need:

pencil

**paper or
3×5 index cards**

Begin by creating a list with the child of 20 to 30 words. You may choose words randomly from a storybook. The child may even want to include words he or she is particularly fond of.

Write the words on index cards or on separate pieces of paper. Then invite the child to make up categories and to sort the word cards into those categories. The child may sort the words by first letter, by last letter, or by meaning, such as things that grow, things that fly, and so on. Encourage the child to choose one category and tell a story using all the words in that category.

Advice for Mother Goose

Help Mother Goose with her plentiful perplexities and problems!

What You'll Need:

**Mother Goose
nursery rhymes
book**

Share one or two nursery rhymes with the child. After the child listens to a rhyme, have him or her describe the difficulties the characters are involved in.

Encourage the child to suggest ideas that the different characters might try (if they could) to solve each of their problems. If it's too late for the characters, let the child suggest what the characters might have done to prevent the problems that occurred!

Word by Word

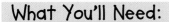

Roll the dice and see who reads the next part of the story!

What You'll Need:

dice

short story

Take turns reading aloud a short story with the child, sentence by sentence. A roll of the dice determines how many sentences each player will read per turn. Begin by rolling the dice to see who goes first—high roll wins. The first player rolls the dice to determine how many sentences he or she should read. The next player rolls the dice and reads the number of sentences that are shown on the dice, starting where the last player left off. This technique helps with vocabulary building, word recall, and patience!

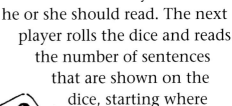

For a challenging twist, try writing a story together, word by word. Roll the dice for each turn to determine how many words of the story a player must contribute.

What the Sunday Funnies Really Say

Make up new stories for old funnies!

What You'll Need:

Sunday newspaper comics

white stick-on labels

pen

 Place white stick-on labels inside the word bubbles of the Sunday funnies. The child can look at the sequence of pictures of a comic and make up a story to go along with the sequence. The child can dictate the words that each character says while you write the words in the bubbles. Read the new story back to the child, or have the child read the story to you.

Stack-a-Story

Busy hands will love the challenge of this story-building activity.

What You'll Need:

3–6 cardboard boxes

poster paints

paintbrush

 Set out boxes and materials for painting. Discuss the main events in a favorite story or a story you and the child have recently read together. Then assist the child in painting a story scene on each cardboard box. When the boxes are dry, have the child stack them in rows so they can be "read" from left to right. Invite the child to retell the story in sequential order.

Quick Draw!

This observation and classification activity will amuse the child endlessly.

What You'll Need:

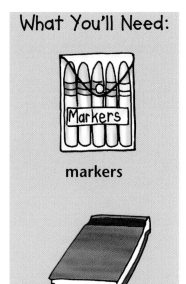

markers

large sheets of paper

Have the child draw four animals (or other objects) on a piece of paper, making sure that three have similar characteristics. The child may want to start with pictures of a zebra, a tiger, a coral snake, and a rabbit. Let the child decide which three are alike and in what ways. You'll notice in the example shown that three have stripes. It is also true that three of the animals shown have four legs.

Challenge the child to "fix" the fourth animal or object to make it be like the other three. Be prepared for some silly drawings!

Look! A Book!

Add to a private library by making a personal book!

What You'll Need:

construction paper

scissors

hole punch

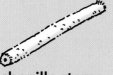

chenille stems

markers

Cut construction paper into equal-size squares. The child can count out five squares of paper and punch a hole in the top left corner of each of the squares. Then the child can loop a chenille stem through the holes and twist the ends.

Time to draw a story in the book and share it! Make blank books ahead of time for just the right moment—when the author is ready to write or draw! Another way to fasten the books is to punch several holes along one edge and weave a chenille stem through the holes.

For a fun variation, create blank books with different shapes. Cut out pages into apple, animal, or house shapes that can be combined into a book. Young authors can create stories to fit the different shapes.

A Box-o'-Socks

Laundry day is awash with this sorting activity that engages the child in critical thinking.

What You'll Need:

box or laundry basket

socks

Collect socks in a variety of sizes, colors, patterns, and types. Check out some used clothing stores if you need a wider variety. Then have the child sort the socks into several specific categories. For example, sort first by color, then by size. Next try sorting by function, such as socks for a baseball player, soccer player, snow skier, or maybe a ballerina. Invite the child to think of new categories for sorting socks. See how many different sorting ideas the child can come up with.

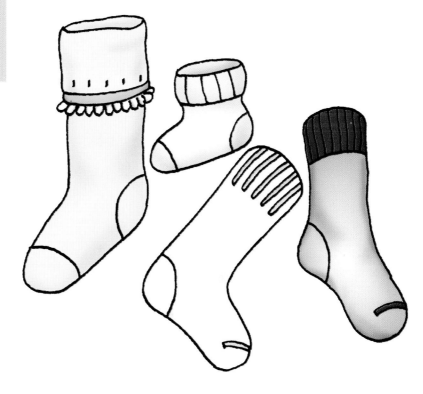

Rebus Recipe

Read and follow a rebus recipe, and end up eating a yummy treat.

What You'll Need:

measuring cup

paper

marker

½ cup peanut butter

¼ cup honey

2½ cups puffed wheat

spoon

bowl

waxed paper

Make a rebus recipe chart for a peanut butter and puffed wheat treat that shows and tells the directions with words and pictures. Use the example shown, or make up your own rebus. After washing up, the child can make the snack!

Following the picture directions, the child can measure the peanut butter, honey, and puffed wheat; mix the ingredients; roll the dough into balls; and place the balls on waxed paper. Then it's time to taste the delicious treat!

Character Interview

Encourage the child to interpret information and make predictions while pretending to be a favorite character.

What You'll Need:

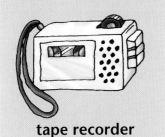

**tape recorder
(optional)**

 Invite the child to pretend to be a favorite character from a favorite story. Explain that you are going to interview the character and that the child should answer all your questions as the character would. Ask questions that wouldn't necessarily be found in the original story. For example, ask the character about favorite foods, what kind of stories the character likes to read, or what the character wants to be when it grows up. If you've recorded the interview, listen to the playback.

After you interview the child/character, choose another character together and switch roles. Now it's the child's turn to interview you!

Legendary Lists

Invent fanciful categories, and fill them with imaginary listings.

What You'll Need:

pen or pencil

paper

Take turns creating categories and challenging one another to name real or pretend events, ideas, or items that fit into them. Encourage the child to have fun and be creative when making the list! Some examples of categories that you might suggest for one another are: important items to take along on a trip to Mars; new holidays that should be invented; unusual ways to use a paper cup; new flavors of ice cream that might be created. For further fun, turn a fanciful list into a story!

News Flash

Invite the child to be a news anchor, recalling events from a favorite story.

What You'll Need:

pen or pencil

paper

Begin by choosing a story the child has read and is familiar with. Then help the child select and organize information, which is an important reading skill needed to retell a story as a newscaster. Next, invite the child to report the events of the story from the point of view of a news reporter.

How would the reporter describe what happened? What would the headline be? Can the child retell the major events of the story as if they were being broadcast on the evening news?

Tracking Down Words

Create a story from words found on a walk, and provide an opportunity for verbal expression.

What You'll Need:

pen or pencil

paper

 Take a walk outside together to track down words. Bring a pen or pencil and paper along, and search for words that are displayed in easy view, such as on a street sign or a billboard. Write down 10 to 20 of the words you discover. When you return, encourage the child to make up a story or narration using the words that you collected together. This activity will also enhance the child's observation and imagination skills.

The inquisitive child will also enjoy searching for 10 to 20 words found inside the house, or in even in just one room!

Funny Days

The calendar will never be the same with this fun, day-renaming activity.

What You'll Need:

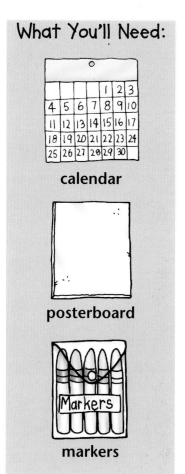

calendar

posterboard

markers

 Before beginning this activity, look at a calendar together with the child and point out the following: the month and year, days of the week, numbers for the days, and special events. After setting out posterboard and markers, invite the child to design a calendar for one week, like the example shown here. Have the child create new names for the days of the week based on his or her scheduled activities or how he or she feels about a particular day. For example, if the child plays soccer on Saturdays, he or she might rename it *Soccerday*; the child's favorite day might be renamed *Funday*.

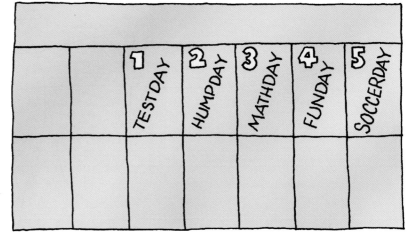

Word Wheel

Get rolling with word play in this activity, and explore words that move.

What You'll Need:

pencil

paper

 Have the child draw a picture of a wheel, using the example shown here as a guide. Be sure to include spokes and a round area in the center. Invite the child to think of something that moves, such as a bicycle, roller blades, or a wheelbarrow. Then have the child write the chosen word in the center of the word wheel. Talk about all the words you can think of that relate to that word. For example, a bicycle may include *handlebars, brakes, seat, gears*, and so on. Have the child write the related words between the spokes as demonstrated below.

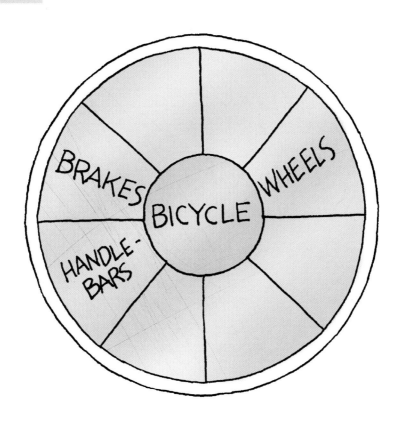

Story Stew

Inspire original storytelling by incorporating common household objects.

What You'll Need:

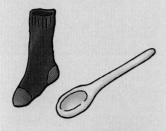

5–7 random household objects (such as a sock, mixing spoon, salt shaker, hat, yarn)

 Choose five to seven common but unrelated household items, and lay them on a table. Challenge the child to make up and tell a silly story that includes each of the items! Encourage the child, as he or she is inventing the story, to add or take away items in order to make the story better, just like a stew!

After the child has created a story, suggest that he or she act out that story, using the items as props.

My Name Is Adam

Here's a challenging game that encourages fast thinking and learning the alphabet.

This alphabet chant game requires the child to think of a name, a place, and an object that begin with the same letter of the alphabet. Start the game at the beginning of the alphabet with the letter *A*. For example, you might begin by saying, "My name is Adam, I come from Alabama, and I like apples." Then invite the child to repeat the chant, replacing each *A* word with an appropriate word that starts with *B*. Then take another turn, moving into *C* words. See how many letters in the alphabet can be turned into chants.

Increase the difficulty of the game by clapping to set a beat. Each time a new sentence is chanted, the child must speak on the beat without stopping to take extra time to come up with the right words.

Sequel Stories

Imagine what happens after the story ends!

What You'll Need:

Favorite folktale or story

 Encourage the child to think about what happens after a favorite story ends. What do the people and animals do next? Do they have any other problems? Adventures? Funny experiences? Do they stay in the same place? Move far away? Go on a vacation? Do they meet any new people? After reading or retelling a favorite story, invite the child to make up and tell a story about what happens after the first story ends!

For a variation, the child can think of a "prequel" rather than a sequel, imagining and making up what took place just before the story in the storybook began.

Word Collage

Words take on a personality all their own when they are artistically arranged in a collage. Get creative!

What You'll Need:

old magazines

scissors

paper

clear tape or glue

Choose a topic. Good examples include food, fashion, sports, and music. Then have the child look through magazines to find all the related words he or she can in headlines or advertisements. Look for words in a variety of type styles, colors, and artistic treatments. Have the child cut out the words. Then invite the child to place the words on a large sheet of paper to create new sentences, phrases, or interesting arrangements. Add appropriate punctuation to enhance the collage. Glue or tape all the words in place. If there is room, the child can add related pictures.

Story Cards

Use interesting pictures to elicit entertaining tales!

What You'll Need:

old magazines

scissors

paper

glue

Encourage the child to choose assorted subjects, such as people, animals, places, foods, shoes, etc., from magazines. The child can then cut out 10 to 12 pictures of these subjects. Glue each picture onto a separate piece of paper to create story cards. When the glue is dry, turn the papers upside down, and spread them out. The child can choose three of the story cards to turn over. After the child has a chance to see the pictures, he or she can make up a story that includes all three of them.

The story cards can also be used for cooperative storytelling. One person can choose a card from the upside-down cards and begin to tell a story about that picture. The next person should choose another card and make up the next part of the story, incorporating that new picture. Keep on turning over new pictures and adding to the story. See where it leads you!

For a twist, use the cards to make a storytelling flip book. Sort the cards into three groups: people or animals, things, and places, then attach them to cardboard backing with brads.

Hanging It Out to Dry

The child can retell a favorite story while hanging homemade socks on a clothesline.

What You'll Need:

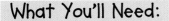

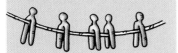
clothesline and clothespins

scissors

tagboard

markers

favorite book or story

 String a clothesline across one corner of the room, and clip several clothespins to it. Next have the child cut out three to six sock shapes from tagboard and, using the markers, illustrate a scene from a familiar story on each. You may wish to provide a copy of the book or story for the child to refer to while working. Then have the child hang the completed socks on the clothesline in sequential order while retelling the story.

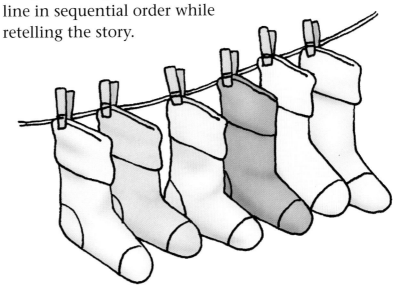

As a fun, bet-I've-got-you-thinking variation of this activity, mix up the socks and hang them in random order on the clothesline. Challenge the child to find the mistake and correct it, or to make up a new story with the events in the new order.

Lights, Camera, Action!

While taking part in dramatizing a favorite story, the child will focus upon story comprehension.

What You'll Need:

hats

masks

costume
props

Begin by choosing a favorite story together that has lots of action. Then act it out together with the child, or invite the child to play all the parts in the story. Use hats, masks, or simple costume props such as scarves and over-size shirts to depict the differ-ent characters.

Character Transplant

Interesting situations prevail when a character is transported from its original story to new surroundings.

What You'll Need:

storybook

Choose a character from a favorite story together. Discuss what the character is like and how he, she, or it acts, reacts, solves problems, and so on. Then create a whole new story or situation, and put that character in it. Invite the child to talk about what the character would do and how the character would react in that entirely new setting.

Chapter 4
Vocabulary Views

One-Syllable Alien

An alien visits Earth to teach young earthlings about one-syllable words.

What You'll Need:

masking tape

markers

box or backpack

index cards

Pretend that an alien lands its spacecraft at the child's school or home. It has come to collect objects to take back to a faraway planet. The alien, however, only collects objects that have one-syllable names. Invite the child to collect one-syllable objects, label them with masking tape, and place them in a backpack or box for easy transporting. Then, using index cards, have the child make a list of one-syllable words, in addition to the objects in the backpack, for the alien to take back to its faraway planet. How many does the child know?

Plant a Root Word

Learning root words has never been more fun than in this planting activity.

What You'll Need:

polystyrene cups

markers

dirt

construction paper

scissors

craft sticks

clear tape or glue

Write a root word on a cup, and then fill the cup with dirt. You may want to use one of the following root words: *fold, do, view, hurt,* or *season.* Invite the child to draw and cut out three to five flowers from construction paper. Help the child glue or tape the paper cutouts onto craft sticks to make them sturdy. Have the child add ending letters (such as *ing* or *er*) or beginning letters (such as *un* or *pre*) to each root word to make new words, writing a new word on each flower. Finished flowers should be "planted" in the cup of dirt. Invite the child to make additional cups of flowers.

Tic-Tac-Toe a Word

Try this new twist on the popular children's game.

What You'll Need:

paper

felt-tip pens

sticky notes

 Make a tic-tac-toe board similar to the one shown below. The spaces should be relatively large, at least 1½×1½ inches. Next decide on nine words, perhaps theme-related words (such as foods, animals, favorite story characters) or recently learned vocabulary words, and write them in random order in the spaces.

Draw an *X* on five sticky notes, and draw an *O* on five different sticky notes. The game is then played as in regular tic-tac-toe, except here the player must say the word in the box he or she chooses and use it in a sentence before covering it with a sticky note. The first player to cover three words in a row—either across, down, or on a diagonal—wins the game.

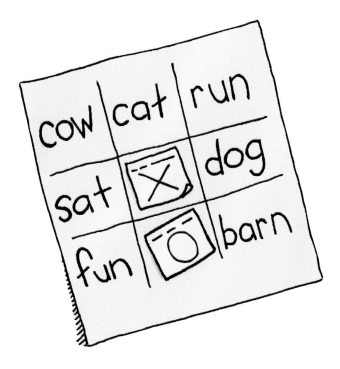

Stick Ups

Forming words from mixed-up letters is an exciting and educational way for the child to learn story vocabulary.

What You'll Need:

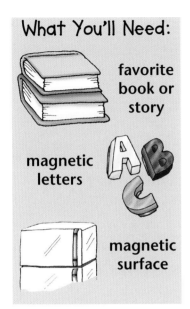

favorite book or story

magnetic letters

magnetic surface

 Select an interesting word from a favorite book or story, and collect magnetic letters to make that word. Use a safe work surface to display the letters, such as a magnetic board, a refrigerator door, the front of a washing machine, or a metal file cabinet. Then scramble the letters. Next, invite the child to unscramble the letters to create the known word. You may want to provide clues to help the child guess the word. Continue the activity with more words from the story.

Word Wall

Let words be a positive experience and a memory booster for the child with this creative activity.

What You'll Need:

large sheets of paper

masking tape

markers

favorite books

Hang several large sheets of paper on a wall. Place a variety of markers nearby. Explain that the child is going to fill the papers with words about books he or she has read, such as quotes, authors' names, titles, and so on. Remind the child how powerful punctuation can be. For example, if he or she really likes an author, the child might write the author's name and follow it with an exclamation point instead of a period.

Syllable Bugs

Creepy, slimy bugs have invaded this syllable activity. Watch out!

What You'll Need:

egg carton

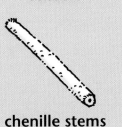

scissors

chenille stems

 To make insect models out of egg cartons, first separate the egg cups by cutting the carton apart. Next ask the child to think of an insect, perhaps a butterfly or a caterpillar. Help the child determine how many syllables are in the word. Then have the child write each syllable of the insect's name on an egg cup, one syllable per cup.

Use short pieces of chenille stems to attach the cups together. Bend and twist additional chenille stems, poking them through the cups, to create antennae, wings, or other features that you and the child would like to add to make the insect look complete. For continued syllabic fun, choose from these other insects: beetle, bumblebee, hornet, centipede, and grasshopper.

Wastepaper Basketball

The child will enjoy hooping it up with this mock basketball activity!

What You'll Need:

wastebasket

masking tape

old magazines

scissors

Mark the floor with masking tape at two distances from the wastebasket; for example, one masking-tape mark might be at four or five feet from the basket and another could be at seven or eight feet.

Explain to the child that a digraph is a combination of two letters that form one sound, such as *sh* or *th*, and invite the child to choose a digraph. Next have the child flip through old magazines to find pictures of objects that begin or end with the chosen digraph. Cut these pictures out. Place each picture that *begins* with the sound at the closer mark to the wastepaper basket. Place each picture that *ends* with the sound at the farther mark. The child can then choose a picture, say the word, and then crumple the paper up and toss it from the appropriate line, trying to make a basket. One point is scored for short shots, two points for long shots.

To vary, label three boxes with digraphs. Have the child toss crumpled blank paper into the boxes, scoring 1 point for a hit and 2 points for naming a word that using that box's labeled digraph.

Invisible Words

Spies and detectives have used this clever writing trick for years.
Here's the secret recipe!

What You'll Need:

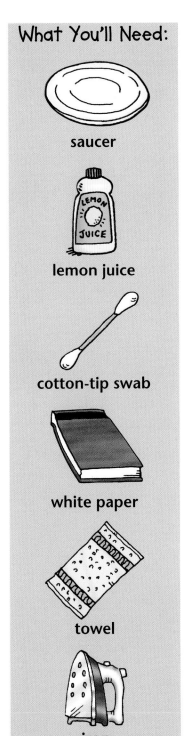

saucer

lemon juice

cotton-tip swab

white paper

towel

iron

Pour some lemon juice into a saucer. Invite the child to dip a cotton-tip swab into the lemon juice and write a sentence, or message, on white paper. Perhaps the child can use new spelling words in the sentence. Then watch. As the juice dries, the writing becomes virtually invisible! Next, have the child give you the invisible message to see if it can be read.

TOP SECRET TIP FOR ADULTS ONLY: To make the words reappear, place the message facedown on top of an old towel or rag. Iron the back of the paper with a warm iron. Share the encoded message with the child, and see how many words are spelled correctly.

Strike!

Have a ball with this simple milk-jug bowling game, designed to reinforce word recognition.

What You'll Need:

**10 plastic milk jugs
(½ gallon or quart)**

permanent markers

rubber ball

 Have the child use permanent markers to write words on the plastic milk jugs. Set up the jugs like bowling pins in rows of one, two, three, and four, as shown. Invite the child to roll a ball down the "lane" and try to knock over the pins. The child gets one point for each pin he or she knocks over—but only after reading the word on it!

Phonics Salad

Toss some phonics in your recipe for a healthy, educational salad!

What You'll Need:

salad ingredients

large bowl

salad spoons

salad dressing

pencil

index card

Explain to the child that there are all sorts of salads, such as vegetable salad, fruit salad, and salad with meat or pasta. Begin by listing all of the ingredients you might put into a salad. Next, make a real salad using only ingredients that have a short vowel sound. For example, suggest a tossed vegetable salad that could have any or all of the following short-vowel ingredients: lettuce, radish, celery, mushroom, egg, asparagus, olive, ham, bell pepper, and any others you can think of. Top the salad with a favorite dressing, and enjoy the finished product! (If you do not want to make a real salad, you can easily adapt this activity to writing the ingredients on a recipe card.)

Mouse in a Blouse

Bet you can't play Mouse in a Blouse without laughing.
Ready, set, try it!

What You'll Need:

paper

pencil

crayons

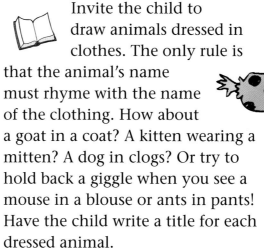

Invite the child to draw animals dressed in clothes. The only rule is that the animal's name must rhyme with the name of the clothing. How about a goat in a coat? A kitten wearing a mitten? A dog in clogs? Or try to hold back a giggle when you see a mouse in a blouse or ants in pants! Have the child write a title for each dressed animal.

Color Words

Making books about color is a fun and productive way for the child to reinforce color words.

What You'll Need:

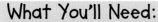

picture book showing color words

paints & brush

paper

pencil

Read a book aloud together. Then read the book again, pointing out the color words on the pages. Talk about how the illustrator and/or author used color and words to show what the words, such as *red*, mean. Together, think of some ideas and pictures that might appear in a book. Then invite the child to use paints to make that book. If the child is just learning to write, help the child print the color words to label the colors.

Peek-a-Boo

Wits will be sharpened with this brainteasing and thinking activity.
Get ready!

What You'll Need:

list of vocabulary words

paper

pen or pencil

sticky notes

 Review a list of vocabulary words with the child. These may be words used in math, science, social studies, or reading. Write a sentence for each vocabulary word on the list. Then cover the vocabulary word in each sentence with a sticky note. Invite the child to read the sentences and try to determine which word is under the flap before lifting it and peeking to check.

What strategies did the child use to discover the word? Emphasize how listening to the other words in the sentence and thinking about words that will make sense in completing the sentence is a good strategy for finding the missing word.

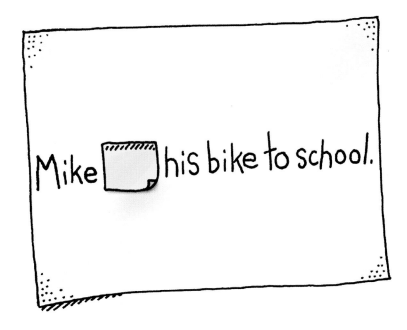

Doggie, Doggie

Defining words is not so r-r-r-rough when the child is engaged in this dog-and-bone game.

What You'll Need:

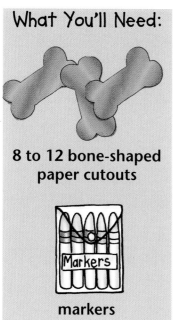

8 to 12 bone-shaped paper cutouts

markers

Write vocabulary words on bone-shaped cutouts. Sit on the floor facing each other to play the game "Doggie, Doggie, Who's Got Your Bone?" While one player chants, "Doggie, doggie, who's got your bone?" the other player sits with the bones turned over so that the writing is facedown. When the "doggie" finishes the chant, he or she picks up one of the bones and reads the word. If the "doggie" can correctly define the word, he or she keeps the bone, and play continues. If not, the "doggie" must give the other player a chance to collect some bones.

Stamp It!

All the child needs to make and send this special birthday card is a little word study and a lot of love.

What You'll Need:

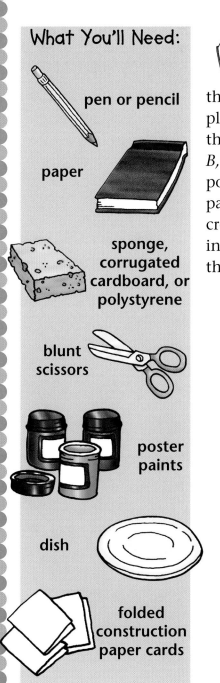

pen or pencil

paper

sponge, corrugated cardboard, or polystyrene

blunt scissors

poster paints

dish

folded construction paper cards

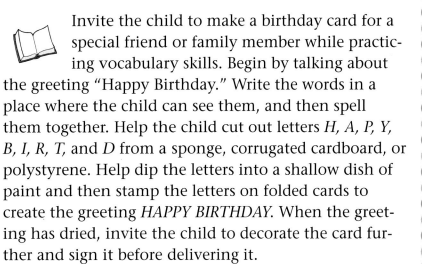

Invite the child to make a birthday card for a special friend or family member while practicing vocabulary skills. Begin by talking about the greeting "Happy Birthday." Write the words in a place where the child can see them, and then spell them together. Help the child cut out letters *H, A, P, Y, B, I, R, T,* and *D* from a sponge, corrugated cardboard, or polystyrene. Help dip the letters into a shallow dish of paint and then stamp the letters on folded cards to create the greeting *HAPPY BIRTHDAY*. When the greeting has dried, invite the child to decorate the card further and sign it before delivering it.

Mark It!

The child will enjoy reading with you while learning about beginning sounds. Pull up a chair!

What You'll Need:

favorite picture book

sticky notes

pen or pencil

Choose a favorite picture book with the child. Then have the child write one consonant on each of five separate sticky notes. While the child pages through the picture book, ask him or her to mark with a sticky note five objects or words in the book that use the corresponding consonant. Invite the child to share the book with you, pointing out the words and pictures he or she has marked.

Long Vowel Hunt

In the cupboard? In the toy box? Who knows where the child will find objects needed for this vowel hunt.

What You'll Need:

construction paper

markers

Fold a large piece of paper into five columns. Write these headings at the top: "Long A," "Long E," "Long I," "Long O," "Long U." Review these sounds together. Next have the child walk around the room, the house, or outside in the yard in search of objects that contain one of these vowel sounds. Ask the child to find at least three objects for each long vowel. Have the child write the name of each object he or she finds in the appropriate column on the paper.

Word-a-Day

Learn new words every day of the week with this "drip-dry" method.

What You'll Need:

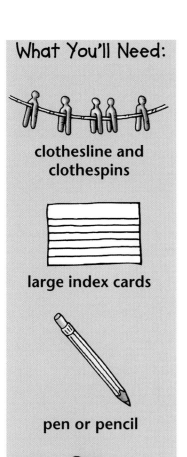

clothesline and clothespins

large index cards

pen or pencil

clothesline pouch (zipper bag, drawstring sack, or other container)

 String a clothesline across one corner of the room, and clip clothespins along the line. Next, write interesting theme-related words on index cards. Choose words such as *caterpillar, cocoon,* and *butterfly* (from a science project), or *square, circle,* and *triangle* (from a math lesson on shapes). Place the words in the clothesline pouch.

Each day, invite the child to pick a word from the pouch. Help the child say the word, use it in a sentence, and illustrate it when applicable. Then have the child clip the new word to the clothesline to review later.

Mischief Makers

A little word mischief will add just the right amount of intrigue and excitement to vocabulary building.

What You'll Need:

large index cards or sticky notes

markers

clear tape

 Invite the child to make labels for different objects in the room, such as doors, cabinets, computers, and so on. Have the child stick or tape the labels beside or on the corresponding objects. After a few days, secretly mix up some of the labels. Then tell the child that the labels have been moved by a mystery mischief maker, and encourage him or her to return them to their correct places.

Star Mobile

Star light, star bright, the first star the child sees tonight will be from this attractive vowel mobile.

What You'll Need:

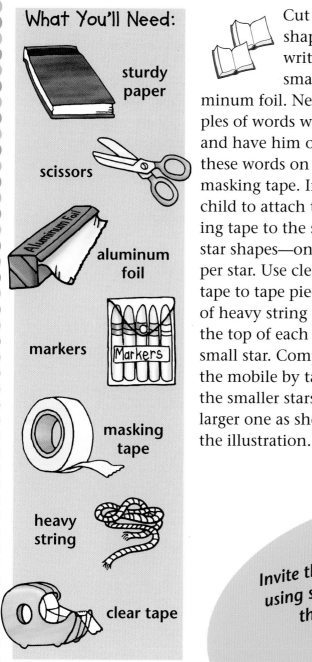

sturdy paper

scissors

aluminum foil

markers

masking tape

heavy string

clear tape

Cut a piece of sturdy paper into a large star shape, cover it with aluminum foil, and write the word *star* on it. Then cut several small star shapes, covering each with aluminum foil. Next invite the child to find other examples of words with the letter pattern *ar* and have him or her write each of these words on a piece of masking tape. Invite the child to attach the masking tape to the smaller star shapes—one word per star. Use clear tape to tape pieces of heavy string to the top of each small star. Complete the mobile by taping the smaller stars to the larger one as shown in the illustration.

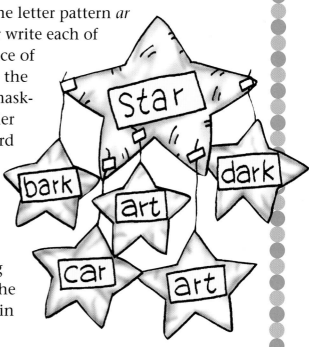

Invite the child to make other mobiles using shapes and words that contain the following letter patterns:

bird

letter

horse

purse

ir

er

or

ur

Marshmallow Models

Marshmallow models are a creative way to learn about letter sounds.
And cleanup is a cinch!

What You'll Need:

pencil

paper

marshmallows

toothpicks

Help the child list objects that begin with a targeted sound, perhaps those created with a silent letter, such as *kn* or *wr*. The objects might include knights, a wrench, or some other object of interest. Then set out marshmallows and toothpicks. Demonstrate how to connect marshmallows with toothpicks before inviting the child to help build models of the objects. Follow up by having the child write about his or her marshmallow model while eating some of the remaining marshmallows.

For a tasty written variation, suggest that the child make a marshmallow model of a written word, creating letters out of marshmallows and toothpicks.

Tree of Words

Try this activity when trees are colorful in the fall or when they are just beginning to sprout new leaves in the spring.

What You'll Need:

notebook

pencil

large piece of paper

CRAYONS

crayons

Begin by taking a walk with the child, talking about the trees in the neighborhood. Take along paper and pencil, and have the child write down all the words related to *tree* that you use, such as *branch, leaves*, or *trunk*. Next, draw a big tree on a large piece of paper, including branches and leaves. Then invite the child to write the tree words in their correct location on the tree. After everything's labeled, suggest that the child color the picture.

LEAVES

TRUNK

BRANCH

Vary this activity by using all the words relating to flowers, such as smell, petal, stem, or bug.

Plenty of Pasta

This clever approach to writing new sight words will have the child practically glued to the paper.

What You'll Need:

heavy paper

alphabet pasta

glue

Invite the child to use alphabet pasta to write new vocabulary words. Have the child select pasta letters and arrange them in order to spell words. Help the child glue the letters on heavy paper. When the glue is dry, the child can trace the letters with his or her fingers and say the words. Encourage the child to use the words in sentences, too.

What's It Mean?

Listen and listen again to find a word's meaning!

Choose a word or word phrase that the child is not familiar with for this sleuthing game. Tell the child the word but not its meaning. Then use the word in a sentence that gives a clue to the meaning of the word. Continue to make up new sentences using the word in different ways until the child is able to figure out what it means! Start off with easy words (for example, *shoe, chair*). Increase the difficulty by using less concrete words, but words that the context will give strong clues to (*lazy*).

Rub-a-Dub-Dub

Invite the child to rub-a-dub-dub objects with a specific sound to make an attractive piece of art.

What You'll Need:

paper bag or cardboard box

newsprint

pencil

Take a nature walk with the child. Bring along a collection bag or box, newsprint, and a pencil. While walking, ask the child to look for objects that have a target sound, such as long *e*. The child should place each of these objects in the collection bag until he or she has at least five things. Help the child arrange the objects on a flat, hard surface. Then cover the collection with newsprint, and invite the child to rub over the top carefully with a pencil. The result will be an interesting print. Invite the child to complete the print by labeling each object on the paper. You may wish to mat the prints and display them in a prominent place.

Chapter 5
Words and More Words

ABC Action

A, B, C, D, E, F, Gee, it's fun to pantomime action words with this up-and-at-'em action activity.

What You'll Need:

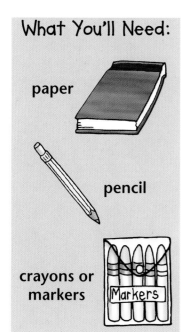

paper

pencil

crayons or markers

What do the words *run, skip, climb, eat, plant, fly,* and *sing* have in common? They are action words, or verbs. Make a list of action words together with the child, then ask the child to choose a word from the list to pantomime. After he or she has acted out the word, invite the child to illustrate the action by writing the word on a piece of paper, making the first letter perform the action. For example, a child may write the word *sing* in which the *s* looks as if it is singing, or write the word *run* in which the *r* appears to be running.

Antonym Checkers

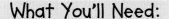

Use antonyms in this challenging game of checkers, and see how many kings you can crown.

What You'll Need:

24×24-inch posterboard or cardboard square

crayons

checkers or large red and black buttons

masking tape

This game is played much like the original game of checkers, except that in order to be "crowned," a player must land on a space with an antonym corresponding to the word on the checker. For example, a player must move a checker marked "lovely" toward and must eventually land on the red space marked "ugly" (the antonym of *lovely*) in order for that checker to be crowned. As in the original game, the player with the last remaining checker wins.

Begin by helping the child make a checkerboard. Draw an 8×8-square grid on a piece of posterboard or cardboard. Color the spaces red and black, alternating the colors as you go. Print the following words in the red squares on the first row of each player's home side: *big, sad, ugly, well*. Before starting the game, invite the child to select the color of checkers he or she would like to use as game pieces.

Next, make two sets of game pieces. For each set, mark the game pieces by putting a piece of masking tape over each checker and writing one of the following words on each: *little, small, tiny, happy, joyful, glad, pretty, lovely, beautiful, ill, sick, unhealthy*. Then set the checkers on the red squares at each end of the board, and you're ready to go. Change the words periodically for continued play.

Create-o-Saurus

Create your very own noun with this word-origin activity.

What You'll Need:

paper

crayons

 Write the words *brontosaurus, tyrannosaurus,* and *stegosaurus* on a piece of paper. Then ask the child: What do all these words have in common? (They are all dinosaurs and nouns, and they all contain the word part *saurus*.) Explain that *saurus* means large lizard. Encourage creative thinking by having the child create and draw new dinosaurs and name them. Remind him or her to use the word part *saurus* in the dinosaur name.

Cowosaurus

Steve Sings and Shouts

Children will love this action-packed verb game, and it will strengthen their imagination.

What You'll Need:

paper

pen or pencil

 Have the child write the first letter of his or her name. Then invite the child to write as many verbs, or action words, as he or she can think of that begin with that same letter. As a follow-up to the activity, see how many nouns—names of people, places, or things—the child can list beginning with that letter.

Poem Pyramids

Practice learning initial sounds of words with these simple sound poems.

What You'll Need:

paper

pen or pencil

 The structure for these sound poems is very simple. Each poem has only four lines. The first line has one word, the second line has two, the third line has three, and the fourth line has four. Each line includes the words of the line before it and adds one new word. The tricky part is that all words must begin with the same letter! Take a look at the example below.

Begin by choosing a letter or inviting the child to choose a letter, and create a poem pyramid together. After finishing the first poem, invite the child to create a new poem independently, using a different letter.

Example:

Bee
Buzzy Bee
Big Buzzy Bee
Big Buzzy Bee Bumbling

Caterpillar Menu

This delicious activity just may become a favorite for the child.

What You'll Need:

A book about food

index cards

markers

paper

Have you ever seen a caterpillar eating a leaf? It seems like the caterpillar will go right through it, eating anything in its way! Read a favorite book about food together with the child. Write all the food words found in the book on the index cards. Which of these foods do you think a caterpillar would like to eat?

Read the book again. This time match the words on the cards to the pages where they appear in the book. Invite the child to arrange the words in the same order they are found in the book. Then create a menu for a caterpillar together, listing all the foods from the book the child thinks the caterpillar might like to eat.

Fishing for Rhymes

Practice identifying rhymes when playing this modified version of Go Fish.

What You'll Need:

30 index cards

crayons or markers

Use index cards to create a deck of rhyming cards. The deck should be made up of 15 rhyme pairs, such as *cat/hat*, *bug/rug*, and *car/star*—one word for each card, 30 cards in all. When the deck is complete, pass out four cards to each player. Explain that the object of the game is to be the first person to get two pairs of rhyming cards.

Begin the game by asking the child for a card that rhymes with a card in your hand. For example, if you have a *hat* card, you would ask, "Do you have a rhyme for *hat*?" If the child has a card that rhymes, he or she must give up that card. If not, you may draw a new card from the deck. For

every card picked from the deck, one must be discarded and placed at the bottom of the deck.

Once the game is finished, encourage the child to create sentences that use a pair of rhymes.

Crossword Puzzles

Across, down, this way and that, crossword puzzles make spelling old hat.

What You'll Need:

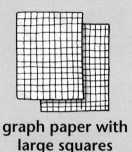

graph paper with large squares

blank paper

pencil

Invite the child to create a crossword puzzle using spelling words you and the child have chosen. The words may be from a list of words the child has had difficulty spelling in daily writing, a spelling list from school, or new words the child wants to learn to spell. Help the child make the words fit on the graph paper, going across or down. Cross as many words at the letters they share as possible. On a separate sheet of paper, assist the child in making a blank puzzle to match the one he or she already created. Then, help the child think of a clue for each word and write those on the bottom of the paper. Be sure to add numbers to the boxes and the clues. The child should then color in the boxes that will be empty. When the puzzle is finished, pass it on to another person to solve.

Extend this activity by turning the answer page on the original graph paper into a word search. Have the child fill each empty square with a letter, surrounding the words already there. A friend can then search for the newly hidden words.

My Body and Me

Combine art and writing while the child learns his or her body size and parts.

What You'll Need:

butcher paper

pencil

scissors

sticky notes

 Begin by placing a large piece of butcher paper, big enough for the child to lay on, on the floor. Then take a pencil and trace around the child. Next, use scissors to cut out the outline carefully. Have the child write the names of body parts on sticky notes and then place the notes at the appropriate parts of the drawing.

Vary this activity by having the child lay on the paper in amusing poses, such as that of a weight lifter. Have the child draw accessories that would go with the chosen pose. In the case of the weight lifter, the child could add barbells. Another variation includes adding clothes for different types of weather, such as a pair of shorts, a coat, or a hat. Lay the clothing on a clean sheet of paper, and trace its outline as well. The child can then label the clothing. "Dress" the body parts depending on the weather.

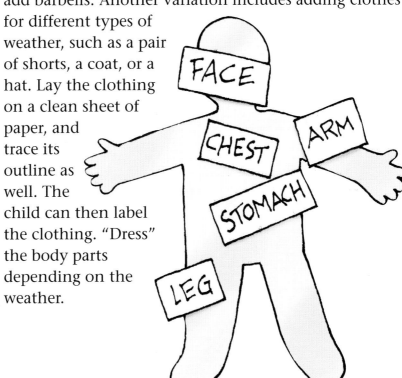

Pasta Mosaic

You can never have too much pasta, right? How many different kinds of pasta do you know?

What You'll Need:

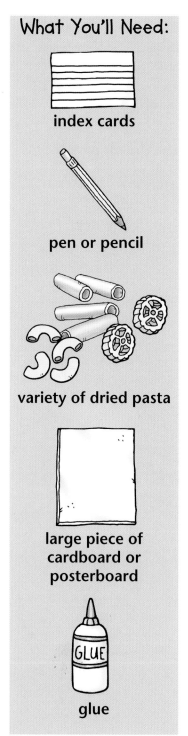

index cards

pen or pencil

variety of dried pasta

large piece of cardboard or posterboard

glue

Choose a variety of words that relate to pasta. Some possibilities might be *sauce, cheese, tomato, spaghetti*, and *macaroni*. Write the words on index cards. Use the pasta to create the words, using different shapes, colors, and types to make the words look interesting. Experiment with the placement of the pasta on the cardboard before gluing it into place. Use the cards to practice reading the words.

Prefix Slip

Create a bevy of different words with this charming approach to prefixes.

 Help the child cut two horizontal slits in the rectangle of tagboard, just above and below the center and slightly toward the right. The slits should be about four inches long and two inches apart. Then have the child write a prefix in the space to the left of the slits as shown. Common prefixes include but are not limited to: *un, re, dis, pre, de,* and *ex.* Help the child brainstorm a list of words that can be added to the prefix to form a new word. Write these words on a strip of paper. Explain that by pulling the strip through the slits, the child can make and read new words with the designated prefix.

Try making another prefix slip, this time writing a common word to the left of the slits, and different prefixes on the paper strip.

Word Walk

Use the great outdoors to encourage good listening and the writing of words associated with all the sounds you hear.

What You'll Need:

clipboard

paper

pencil

Take a walk in your neighborhood. Have the child listen carefully to all the sounds you hear and write them down. Some may not really be words and have no regular spelling. In that case, have the child try to make up a spelling that seems logical, such as *zwee* for a whistle or *fawish* for a breeze. Explain that sometimes these made-up words become real words (this is called *onomatopoeia*, which means the spelling of the word is based on the vocal imitation of the sound).

Label It!

By using labels, the child will identify and learn new words.

What You'll Need:

posterboard

markers or crayons

sticky notes

Explain to the child that pictures make it easier for us to understand a story or any other information that we read. Also explain that some pictures have labels, or captions, next to them to name the parts of a picture. Invite the child to draw a picture of a favorite toy and label the parts he or she knows with sticky notes.

Ice-Cream Syllables

Scoop up a triple-decker treat when you make your own ice-cream syllables.

What You'll Need:

scissors

construction paper

pen or pencil

GLUE

glue

Cut out triangle-shaped cones and round ice-cream scoops from construction paper. Write root words (such as *end, cap,* and *vent*), prefixes (such as *un* or *pre*), which go before a root word, and suffixes (such as *ed* or *ing*), which go after a root word, on the scoops.

Next, invite the child to make triple-decker syllable treats by combining the scoops and gluing or taping them on top of the paper ice-cream cone to make a word. Challenge the child to see if he or she can use the new word in a sentence.

For an extra challenge, have the child make up or write a story including four different ice-cream-cone words, each one used in its own sentence.

Beep! Beep!

Investigate what makes common sounds and experiment with ways to write them.

What You'll Need:

tape recorder

butcher paper

paint

paintbrush

Take a walk outside to record environmental sounds, such as a car horn honking, birds chirping, sirens blaring, the wind howling, dogs barking, and so on. Later, have the child listen to the recorded sounds and create words to describe them. Some examples might include: *beep! beep!, chirp! chirp!, woof! woof!,* and *wr-r-r!* Invite the child to paint the sound words in large letters on long pieces of butcher paper to create a vocabulary mural.

Word Search

Track down and recognize words all around!

What You'll Need:

old magazines

scissors

paper

pencil

box

butcher paper

masking tape

When you walk around the house or the neighborhood, challenge the child to find words that he or she can read. These might be words that the child can sound out and read or words that the child recognizes (like *milk* or *stop*). The child can start a collection of pictures and labels of recognizable words cut out from old magazines. The saved words can be kept in a box or could be used for a word collage. As a variation, you can also start a "Word Wall," where you list all the words the child can read. (Don't actually write on a wall, however! Tape a large piece of butcher paper to the wall and write the words on it.) As the list grows, the child will feel great accomplishment!

Pease Porridge What?

An old nursery rhyme becomes the spark for a study of antonyms.

What You'll Need:

paper

pencil

Repeat the following Mother Goose rhyme, "Pease Porridge Hot." Help the child write down the words to the rhyme. Underline the words *hot* and *cold*. Ask the child how these words are related. (They are opposites.) Invite the child to substitute different pairs of word opposites, or antonyms, to make a silly version of the rhyme.

Pease porridge hot,

pease porridge cold.

Pease porridge in the pot

nine days old.

Some like it hot,

some like it cold.

Some like it in the pot

nine days old.

Why do we remember nursery rhymes and other poems? Because of the rhyme! Have the child decipher the rhyme scheme (the order of the rhymed words) in this and other favorite nursery rhymes. HINT: The rhyme scheme here is ABABABAB.

Compound Caterpillars

The child will enjoy this interesting take on compound words while making construction-paper caterpillars.

What You'll Need:

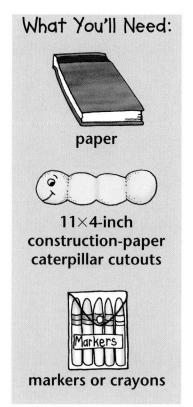

paper

11×4-inch
construction-paper
caterpillar cutouts

markers or crayons

Explain that a compound word is made up of two separate words that are combined to make one word. Take turns naming compound words. Write the words you've named on a chart. Then set out precut paper caterpillars, similar to those shown here. The child can fold the left and right ends of the caterpillar cutouts so that they meet at the middle. Have the child take a particular compound word from the chart and write the smaller words that are a part of it on the outside flaps of the cutout—one word for each flap. Next, have the child unfold the flaps and write the compound word on the inside of the caterpillar. Invite the child to share the finished work with others.

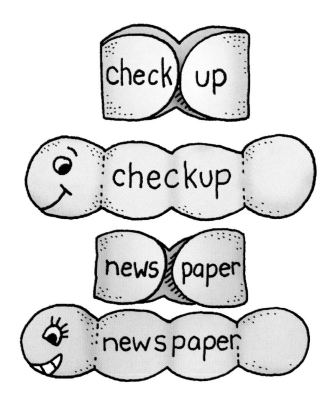

Word Stairs

Enhance the child's ability to build words, step by step.

What You'll Need:

pencil

paper

Begin by having the child write one vocabulary word across the bottom of a piece of paper. Encourage the child to check the spelling of the word by looking up the word in a dictionary, checking it on a computer spell checker, finding it in a book or magazine, or confirming the spelling with you or another adult.

To build the next step in the word stairs, the child must think of a word that ends with the same last letter as the first word. The new word should be written vertically on the paper as shown. The third word must begin with the same first letter as the second word and should be written across the page. Continue this process until a staircase of words has been created from the bottom to the top of the paper. Use a large piece of paper, and challenge the child see how high he or she can build a staircase.

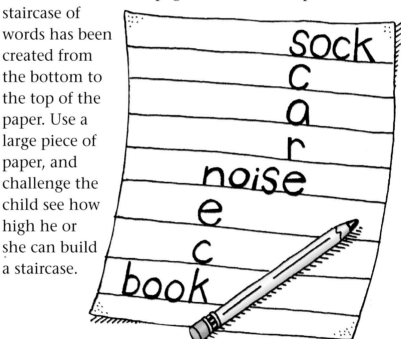

Cheery Chains

Strengthen the child's vocabulary chain by learning new words associated with a familiar topic.

What You'll Need:

1½×8½-inch paper strips

crayons or markers

clear tape or glue

Decide on a topic, such as food, animals, household objects, or the child's current social studies or science theme at school, and make a list of associated words. Then have the child write the words on strips of paper. The child may also want to draw illustrations to go with each word. Be sure to provide the child with glossaries, dictionaries, textbooks, and other materials as spelling aids.

Next, invite the child to assemble the strips, or links, using tape or glue to make chains. Take a strip of paper, and form it into a loop. Tape the ends together. Continue adding loops of paper, stringing each new loop onto the previous one before taping it shut. Chains can be strung across a room, made into individual necklaces, wrapped around bushes or trees, or draped around a doorway. To reinforce learning, invite the child to review the words daily.

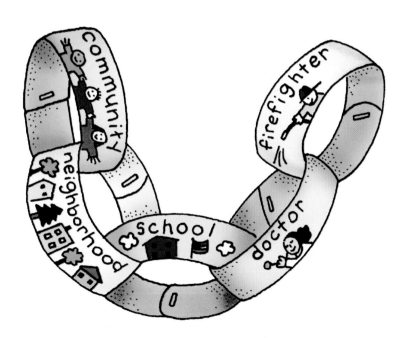

Shoe Sole Word

By matching these shoe soles, the child will practice "stepping into" words.

What You'll Need:

heavy paper precut in shoe-sole shapes

felt-tip pen

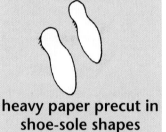

Spelling List
man
car
door
cat

list of spelling words

several pairs of shoes

On pairs of precut paper soles, write words, such as *man*, *car*, and *door*—the same word on each half of the pair. Place one "sole" of each word inside one shoe from each pair so that the card is standing on end and the word is clearly visible. Set out the remaining soles and invite the child to place them in the empty shoe of the pair that matches the one with the same word.

Invented Words

The child will Zam! Pow! and Whammy! into spelling with this awesome cartoon lover's activity.

What You'll Need:

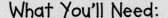

comic strips

paper

crayons

pencil

Review comic strips together, reading and enjoying the action. Look for words made up by the writer or artist that express actions or feelings. Have the child cut out the action words and study them to discover the interesting ways in which they are spelled.

Next, have the child make up his or her own comic words. Invite the child to make a cartoon with the invented words by writing the words in large, colorful letters on construction paper.

Invite the child to create his or her own comic strip by drawing favorite or made-up characters to accompany the comic words.

Shape Words

Draw shape words that illustrate the meaning of nouns.

What You'll Need:

markers or crayons

paper

 Have the child choose words that are nouns, such as insects, animals, or toys. Encourage creative thinking as the child writes the words so that the letters conform to the shape of the object. For example, the letters *c-a-t-e-r-p-i-l-l-a-r* may be written to take on the curved shapes of the insect, as in the example shown, or the word *k-i-t-e* may be written with tall letters to create a diamond shape. What other words can the child decorate?

Chapter 6
Ready for Writing

Going to the Zoo

You can create an exciting zoo and help your child's writing at the same time with this activity.

What You'll Need:

stuffed animals

3×5 index cards

pen or pencil

empty boxes

scissors

tape

Help the child collect a variety of stuffed animals. Then have the child write each animal's name on an index card. Next, take several empty boxes and cut out a window in each box. Place each animal in a box and have the child tape the card with the animal's name under the window.

For a more challenging activity, have the child include background information about the animal. Extend this activity by writing directions for visitors and creating a "map" of the zoo with a list of the animals they will see.

BEN THE BEAR

"I Remember" Poem

This activity is perfect for sharing an unforgettable memory with a favorite relative or friend.

What You'll Need:

paper

pencil or markers

When a special occasion is approaching, such as a birthday, Mother's Day, or Father's Day, have the child think of all the memories he or she can recall about time shared with the person to be celebrated. Invite the child to write down a word or two about each memory. Then have the child create a series of sentences. Most of the sentences should begin with "I remember..." Arrange the sentences into a poem.

I remember when I loved to read in my dad's office.

I remember that there was just enough room between his bookshelves for me to curl up.

I remember that it was always quiet there.

But most of all

I remember that the heater kept me warm!

Suggest that the child write other poems following this format. You might use sentences beginning, "I love...", "I wish...", "I'm happy when...", or other combinations.

Peek-a-Boo Pictures

This observation activity will encourage the child to see "the big picture!"

What You'll Need:

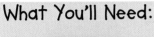

old magazine

scissors

paper

clear tape or glue

 Create peek-a-boo pictures by cutting a picture from an old magazine and gluing or taping it onto a sheet of paper. Do not let the child see the picture. Next, cut a small circle or square in a second piece of paper. This will be the guessing page. Take the guessing page and lay it on top of the picture. The small portion of the picture viewed through the peek-a-boo hole becomes the clue for the child to guess the identity of the bigger picture.

Biography Book Jacket

Writing words for a book jacket is a creative exercise that teaches the child summarization skills.

What You'll Need:

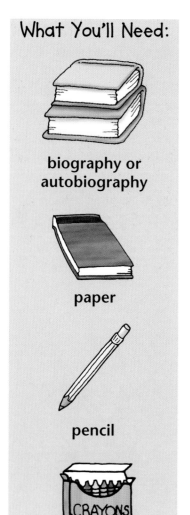

biography or autobiography

paper

pencil

crayons or markers

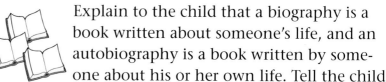

Explain to the child that a biography is a book written about someone's life, and an autobiography is a book written by someone about his or her own life. Tell the child that a book jacket protects the book but sometimes also contains a summary of the book. Look at other book jackets together, and see how those summaries were written. Then have the child read a biography or autobiography, or read the book together. After the child has finished, discuss the key events in the person's life that were discussed in the biography. Invite the child to write a summary. Use the summary to create a book jacket for the biography or autobiography. Encourage the child to be creative in designing the front of the book jacket.

For an added challenge, invite the child to write a summary that might appear on the book jacket of his or her own biography.

Family Newsletter

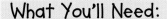

Start a new family tradition that benefits everyone, especially if family members live far apart.

What You'll Need:

pencil

paper

envelope

stamp

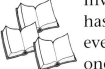

Invite the child to create a newsletter that has one or more short articles about family events. The newsletter can be as simple as one page written in pencil or as elaborate as a booklet done on a computer, complete with special fonts and art. Then have the child send the newsletter to a relative, along with a list of other relatives' addresses and the route the newsletter should take after the first relative reads it. Make sure the final address belongs to the child. A note asking all recipients to add their news to the newsletter should also be enclosed.

When the newsletter returns to the child, he or she should replace the information in the old newsletter with new information. Then the child can send it off again, following the same route as the first edition of the newsletter, and instructing family members to replace their previously circulated information with new information. This way everyone gets the latest family news without having to write individual letters to family members.

Story Play

Stuffed animals and simple stories combine perfectly to give the child an opportunity to develop simple scripts.

What You'll Need:

stuffed animals

simple story

paper

pencil

Ask the child to gather a variety of stuffed animals. Then share a simple story with the child, and discuss how that story can be acted out with the stuffed animals. Make a list of characters together, and plan which animal will play which character. Help the child write the story script form. For rehearsal, read the script aloud while the animals act out the story. Revise the script as necessary until the performance is perfected. Prepare the play, and share it with others.

When the child has the play just right, suggest he or she use a cardboard box for a backdrop, creating scenery by painting different scenes on the different sides.

Acrostic Poetry

This easy form of poetry can be used whenever a special day, person, or event calls for a poem.

What You'll Need:

paper

markers

Perhaps it is Father's Day and the child needs to make a card. Or maybe a special friend or family member needs a comforting thought. To create an acrostic poem, have the child write a key word, such as *father*, vertically on the left side of the paper. Then, on each line, write a related word that begins with each letter, creating a poem such as the following:

> **F**un
> **A**lways helping
> **T**errific
> **H**elpful
> **E**xciting
> **R**eady

For variety, the child can use two or more words for each line, creating a series of phrases.

Cliff-hanger Stories

*Promote story writing with this favorite form of story—
the old-fashioned cliff-hanger.*

What You'll Need:

piece of paper

pencil

hanger

clothespins

 Explain to the child what a cliff-hanger story is. If possible, rent some old movies that have cliff-hanger episodes, or share a story that leaves the reader wanting more at the end of each chapter. Help the child write a cliff-hanger story, with cliff-hangers at the end of each chapter. Write the cliff-hanger event on a piece of paper, and clip it to a hanger. See how long the child can keep the story going, cliff-hanger after cliff-hanger.

Create a Logo

Create a design that represents a specific idea or image about the creator.

What You'll Need:

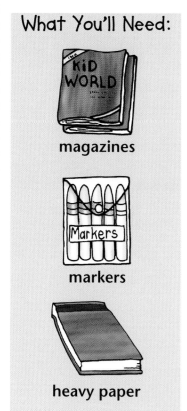

magazines

markers

heavy paper

Explain that a logo is a picture or design intended to tell something about a product that a company wants you to remember. Logos are often accompanied by a few words. Look for examples in magazines or on items you have around the house: sports equipment, electronic equipment, clothing, food, drinks, and so on. Invite the child to design a personal logo that he or she might want to use. The child may wish to use one or more letters in his or her name as part of the design. Each logo should be accompanied by a name the child has created to be used with it. Then think about practical ways to use logos, perhaps to mark possessions or as decorative imprints for clothing.

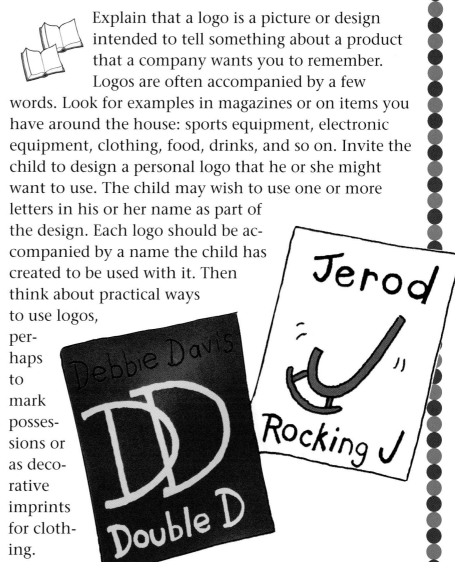

Vocabulary Seed Packets

Little seeds of knowledge can grow into a garden of information with this vocabulary-rich project.

What You'll Need:

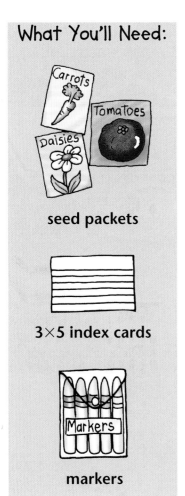

seed packets

3×5 index cards

markers

Have the child look at some real seed packets. Then invite the child to design a seed packet for something they'd like to grow. The plant the child chooses could be real or imaginary. Have the child draw a colorful picture of the plant on the front of an index card and label it. Invite the child to write a descriptive sentence about the plant on the back. The sentence may tell what the plant looks like, explain how or when to plant the seeds, suggest tools needed to do the planting, or remind the grower of foods that can be made from the harvested plant.

The child might also enjoy keeping a seed diary. Have the child wash, dry, and then glue fruit and vegetable seeds onto cards. The child can then label the cards with the name of the seed, date eaten, and comments.

Away We Go

Making a travel brochure will get anyone in the mood to travel!

What You'll Need:

paper

markers

postcards or photographs (optional)

 This activity can be used to plan a trip or to serve as a record of a vacation. If creating the brochure before a trip, use the library to gather information about the destination. You can also go to a travel agency to pick up some sample brochures. Then help the child create his or her own brochure that might convince someone else to choose that destination as a vacation spot.

If you want to do this activity after the child has been to a particular place, you and the child can collect information while on the trip. Invite the child to create the brochure by using postcards or photographs collected on the trip.

Greeting Cards

Build an understanding of an author's purpose, audience, and main idea while creating a friendly greeting.

What You'll Need:

colored construction paper

felt-tip pens

art and craft scraps

clear tape or glue

envelope

stamp

 Discuss a list of greetings together with the child, such as "hello," "get well," "congratulations," "happy birthday," and "I love you." Invite the child to write a greeting on a piece of construction paper and decorate it with art scraps. Then have the child explain who the card is for (audience), why it was made (author's purpose), and what greeting was written (main idea). You may want to assist the child with addressing and stamping the envelopes to mail.

For a fun twist have the child describe the kind of greeting card he or she would enjoy receiving. Then have the child design and write it and then mail it to his or her own home!

PB and J Fun

Warning! This is only for brave adults! Be prepared to be messy!

What You'll Need:

paper

pencil

bread

peanut butter

jelly

knife

plate

Everyone thinks they know how to write good instructions. After all, how hard could it be to write instructions for something as simple as creating a peanut butter and jelly sandwich?

In this activity, invite the child to write instructions for making this favorite sandwich. The child can make as many steps as is necessary. Then you must follow the steps exactly as written. For example, if Step 1 says, "Spread the peanut butter on the bread," you will have to use your fingers for spreading the peanut butter. Nothing was said about using a knife! After the sandwich has been made, discuss the importance of detailed instructions. Have the child rewrite the directions, and try again. *Bon appétit!*

Splash Yourself!

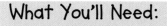

Writing down descriptive words about oneself is a fun and creative way to learn about who we are!

What You'll Need:

pencil

paper

markers or crayons

old magazines (optional)

 Begin this activity by having the child brainstorm descriptive words about who he or she is—such as *smart, kind,* and *fun*—and write them on a piece of paper. Next, have the child write his or her name in the center of a piece of paper. Have the child use markers or crayons to create a "splash" of words or pictures that describe him or herself. This can be extended to include words or pictures cut out from magazines. The child can then use the words to make descriptive sentences.

For variation, have the child make an acrostic poem with his or her name. He or she can find a descriptive word starting with each of the letters in his or her name.

Poster Power

Any child who loves movies or videos will enjoy creating this colorful poster.

What You'll Need:

- news-papers or magazines
- white paper
- pen or pencil
- poster paper
- paints
- paintbrush
- markers or crayons
- scissors
- other decorating materials

 Invite the child to choose a favorite movie or video. Collect information about the star or the movie itself from newspaper or magazine articles, and provide the child with a list of people that includes the stars, the director, the writer, and others involved in the production. Also include other information, such as reviews, that would encourage someone to buy a ticket to see the show. Have the child write a few simple sentences telling what he or she liked about the movie or video.

Next, help the child design the poster. Use paints, crayons, magazine pictures, or other materials to make the poster colorful

and appealing. Display the finished poster in a prominent location.

Taking a Message

Taking a phone message is an important skill and can be taught using this fairy-tale activity.

What You'll Need:

fairy tales

notepaper or pink telephone message forms

pencil

Together with the child, brainstorm several creative phone messages that might have been left by characters from certain fairy tales, such as *Little Red Riding Hood*, *The Three Little Pigs*, or *The Gingerbread Man*. Write these messages on a message pad or on sheets of notepaper. For example, a message from Little Red Riding Hood's mother might read

To: Red

From: Mom

Wolf seen in woods near Grandmother's house. Be careful!

Discuss the difference between the message above and a message that says simply, "Red: Your mom called." Invite the child to come up with new endings to the fairy tales based on what might have happened if the characters had received these telling phone messages. Emphasize the importance of writing down important details and information such as time of call and return telephone number!

To further this activity, encourage the child to practice writing down "messages" as you tell them to him or her.

Sportswriters

*In every sporting event, sportswriters need to be there to get the story.
So grab your pencil!*

What You'll Need:

old newspapers

pencil

paper

scissors

clear tape or glue

newsprint

Invite the child to be a sportswriter. Page through the sports section of a newspaper to familiarize the child with headlines, photo captions, and stories in the sports section. Then help the child collect the tools he or she will need for the next assignment, including a pencil or two, paper, and some newspapers. Explain that the child's task is to capture, in a single sentence, the main idea or most important moment of a sporting event. Explain how important this story is and how it might appear in the sports section of tomorrow's newspaper.

First, have the young sportswriter cut out a picture of someone participating in a sport. Invite the child to write a caption or headline, such as the one pictured here, about the athlete. Glue or tape the headline and picture on newsprint to resemble a newspaper.

Joking Around

Consider "the source" when you need some laughter to liven up your day!

What You'll Need:

stapler

paper

joke books

pencil

 Staple several pieces of paper together to make a book. Go to the library, and check out some joke books. Then have the child write some of the favorite jokes he or she finds in the joke book. The child can also try creating original jokes or revising existing jokes to add to the collection. Share the new joke book with friends and family, and have a constant source of laughter.

Rebus Writing

Test the child's creative thinking, problem-solving skills, and ability to translate pictures into words.

What You'll Need:

construction paper

felt-tip pen

markers

Begin by creating rebus sentences for the child to translate. As you write the sentences, draw certain words, especially repeated words, as pictures. For example, if you wrote a sentence about a king, you could draw a picture of a crown as the symbol for the word *king*. Then challenge the child to translate the rebus sentences you have created. The following is an example to get you started.

Once upon a 🕐, the 👑 visited the 🏰.

It was the 👑's birthday. He ate .

News of the Day!

Explore main ideas as the child writes headlines for a day's events and activities.

What You'll Need:

newspaper

magnetic letters

magnetic surface
(such as refrigerator
door)

Recall the events the child was involved in on a particular day, and discuss the most important and the most memorable. Which event or events would other people want to know about?

Page through a newspaper together. Point out the headlines to the child. Explain that a headline is used to provide a glimpse of what's in the article and entice the reader to read the article.

Display magnetic letters on a magnetic surface. Let the child manipulate the letters freely for a few minutes, then invite the child to arrange the letters to create a headline describing a highlight of the day you discussed earlier.

For an additional challenge, point to a particular headline in the newspaper and ask the child to guess what the story is about. See how accurate the child and the headline are.

Say It in a Letter

Write a letter and send it to someone dear, whether far or near!

What You'll Need:

paper

pencil or markers

envelope

stamp

tape recorder
(optional)

Invite the child to write a letter to a grandparent, relative, friend, or neighbor. The child can dictate the letter to you, or he or she can write independently and use invented spelling to write down ideas if the correct spelling is not known. The child can fold the letter, put it in the envelope, seal it, and put a stamp on it. After you or another adult addresses the letter, the child can decorate the back of the envelope. When the letter is signed, sealed, and ready to go, take a walk together to the nearest mailbox and drop it in! For a variation, next time send a tape-recorded letter. The child can share adventures and news by recording the news and sending off the tape.

The interested child might also enjoy expressing an opinion in a letter to a local official about a community issue, such as a park cleanup or animal rescue.

And Then...

Engaging the child in story sequels stimulates creative thinking and problem solving.

What You'll Need:

favorite book or story

paper

crayons or markers

 Invite the child to reread a favorite book or story and imagine what might occur after the story has ended. What would the characters do next? Would there be another adventure? Will the characters live happily ever after?

Encourage the child to create a sequel to the story and tell or write the next chapter.

Lists, Lists, Lists!

Involve the child in writing a regular household task, such as making a grocery list.

What You'll Need:

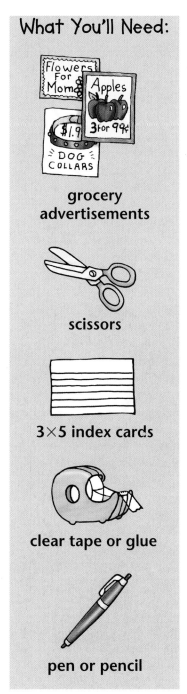

grocery advertisements

scissors

3×5 index cards

clear tape or glue

pen or pencil

 Collect a variety of colorful grocery advertisements that include pictures and words. Have the child cut out the pictures of the grocery items you regularly purchase. Next, the child should glue or tape the pictures to the index cards—one picture per card. Have the child write the word for each item on the other side of the card. Then invite the child to make up a grocery list on a separate card by copying the words from the front of the cards.

Once the child has learned the words, have him or her recall the correct spelling and write the words again using only the pictures. Just for fun, invite the child to make grocery lists for storybook characters, such as Mama Bear from *Goldilocks and the Three Bears* or Little Red Riding Hood. Another good activity is to create lists for special occasions, such as birthdays, holidays, picnics, and so on.

Index

Word and Identification Games

Writing Activities